TEMPLATE ANALYSIS

ANALYSIS

for **BUSINESS** *and* **MANAGEMENT STUDENTS**

SAGE was founded in 1965 by Sara Miller McCune to support the dissemination of usable knowledge by publishing innovative and high-quality research and teaching content. Today, we publish over 900 journals, including those of more than 400 learned societies, more than 800 new books per year, and a growing range of library products including archives, data, case studies, reports, and video. SAGE remains majority-owned by our founder, and after Sara's lifetime will become owned by a charitable trust that secures our continued independence.

Los Angeles | London | New Delhi | Singapore | Washington DC | Melbourne

TEMPLATE ANALYSIS

for BUSINESS and MANAGEMENT STUDENTS

NIGEL KING & JOANNA M. BROOKS

Los Angeles | London | New Delhi
Singapore | Washington DC | Melbourne

Los Angeles | London | New Delhi
Singapore | Washington DC | Melbourne

SAGE Publications Ltd
1 Oliver's Yard
55 City Road
London EC1Y 1SP

SAGE Publications Inc.
2455 Teller Road
Thousand Oaks, California 91320

SAGE Publications India Pvt Ltd
B 1/I 1 Mohan Cooperative Industrial Area
Mathura Road
New Delhi 110 044

SAGE Publications Asia-Pacific Pte Ltd
3 Church Street
#10-04 Samsung Hub
Singapore 049483

Editor: Delia Martinez-Alfonso
Editorial assistant: Lyndsay Aitken
Production editor: Sarah Cooke
Marketing manager: Catherine Slinn
Cover design: Francis Kenney
Typeset by: C&M Digitals (P) Ltd, Chennai, India
Printed and bound by CPI Group (UK) Ltd,
Croydon, CR0 4YY

Library of Congress Control Number: 2016937676

British Library Cataloguing in Publication data

A catalogue record for this book is available from
the British Library

ISBN 978-1-47391-156-7
ISBN 978-1-47391-157-4 (pbk)

At SAGE we take sustainability seriously. Most of our products are printed in the UK using FSC papers and boards.
When we print overseas we ensure sustainable papers are used as measured by the PREPS grading system.
We undertake an annual audit to monitor our sustainability.

CONTENTS

Editors' Introduction   vii
About the Series Editors   ix
About the Authors   xi

1 Introduction   1
2 Philosophical Issues When Using Template Analysis   13
3 Doing Template Analysis: A Guide to the Main Components
   and Procedures   25
4 Case Examples of the Use of Template Analysis   47
5 The Use of Template Analysis in Published Research: The Careers
   Literature as an Exemplar   73
6 Strengths and Limitations of Template Analysis   85

References   95
Index   101

EDITORS' INTRODUCTION TO THE *MASTERING BUSINESS RESEARCH METHODS* SERIES

Welcome to the *Mastering Business Research Methods* series. In recent years, there has been a great increase in the numbers of students reading Master's level degrees across the business and management disciplines. A great number of these students have to prepare a dissertation towards the end of their degree programme in a time-frame of three to four months. For many students, this takes place after their taught modules have finished and is expected to be an independent piece of work. While each student is supported in their dissertation or research project by an academic supervisor, the student will need to find out more detailed information about the method that he or she intends to use. Before starting their dissertations or research projects these students have usually been provided with little more than an overview across a wide range of methods as preparation for this often daunting task. If you are one such student, you are not alone. As university professors with a deep interest in research methods, we have provided this series of books to help students like you. Each book provides detailed information about a particular method to support you in your dissertation. We understand both what is involved in Master's level dissertations, and what help students need with regard to methods in order to excel when writing a dissertation. This series is the only one that is designed with the specific objective of helping Master's level students to undertake and prepare their dissertations.

Each book in our series is designed to provide sufficient knowledge about either a method of data collection or a method of data analysis, and each book is intended to be read by the student when undertaking particular stages of the research process, such as data collection or analysis. Each book is written in a clear way by highly respected authors who have considerable experience of teaching and writing about research methods. To help students find their way around each book, we have utilized a standard format, with each book having been organized into six chapters:

- **Chapter 1** introduces the method, considers how the method emerged for what purposes, and provides an outline of the remainder of the book.
- **Chapter 2** addresses the underlying philosophical assumptions that inform the uses of particular methods.
- **Chapter 3** discusses the components of the relevant method.
- **Chapter 4** considers the way in which the different components may be organized to use the method.
- **Chapter 5** provides examples of published studies that have used the method.
- **Chapter 6** concludes by reflecting on the strengths and weaknesses of that method.

We hope that reading your chosen books helps you in your dissertation.

Bill Lee, Mark N.K. Saunders and Vadake K. Narayanan

ABOUT THE SERIES EDITORS

Bill Lee, PhD, is Professor of Accounting and Head of the Accounting and Financial Management Division at the University of Sheffield, UK. He has a long-standing interest in research methods and practice, in addition to his research into accounting and accountability issues. Bill's research has been published widely, including in: *Accounting Forum, British Accounting Review, Critical Perspectives on Accounting, Management Accounting Research, Omega* and *Work, Employment & Society*. His publications in the area of research methods and practice include the co-edited collections *The Real Life Guide to Accounting Research* and *Challenges and Controversies in Management Research*.

Mark N.K. Saunders, BA MSc PGCE PhD FCIPD, is Professor of Business Research Methods at Birmingham Business School, University of Birmingham, UK. His research interests are research methods, in particular methods for choosing participants and for understanding intra organizational relationships; human resource aspects of the management of change, in particular trust within and between organizations; and small and medium-sized enterprises. Mark's research has been published in journals including *British Journal of Management, Journal of Small Business Management, Field Methods, Human Relations, Management Learning* and *Social Science and Medicine*. He has co-authored and co-edited a range of books including *Research Methods for Business Students* (currently in its seventh edition) and the *Handbook of Research Methods on Trust* (currently in its second edition) and the *Handbook of Research Methods on Human Resource Development*.

Vadake K. Narayanan, BA MA PhD, is the Associate Dean for Research, Director of the Center for Research Excellence, and the Deloitte Touché Stubbs Professor of Strategy and Entrepreneurship in Drexel University, Philadelphia, Pennsylvania. His articles have appeared in leading professional journals such as *Academy of Management Journal, Academy of Management Review, Accounting Organizations and Society,*

Journal of Applied Psychology, *Journal of Management*, *Journal of Management Studies*, *Management Information Systems Quarterly*, *R&D Management* and *Strategic Management Journal*. Narayanan holds a bachelor's degree in mechanical engineering from the Indian Institute of Technology, Madras, a postgraduate degree in business administration from the Indian Institute of Management, Ahmedabad, and a PhD in business from the Graduate School of Business at the University of Pittsburgh, Pennsylvania.

ABOUT THE AUTHORS

Nigel King is Professor in Applied Psychology at the University of Huddersfield, UK. He has a long-standing interest in the use of qualitative methods in real-world research. With a background in both organizational and health psychology, his research interests include professional identities and interprofessional relations in health and social care. He is author with Christine Horrocks of *Interviews in Qualitative Research* (SAGE, 2010) and with Neil Anderson of *Managing Innovation and Change: A Critical Guide for Organizations* (Thomson Learning, 2002). Nigel is well-known for his work on Template Analysis and, more recently, the development of a visual interview technique known as 'Pictor'.

Dr Joanna Brooks is Senior Research Fellow in the Centre for Applied Psychological and Health Research at the University of Huddersfield, UK. Her primary research interests focus on applied research topics in healthcare, social care and education settings. Jo has a particular interest in using qualitative research to explore interpersonal factors in the management and experience of chronic illness conditions.

1

INTRODUCTION

Qualitative research is at heart about people as meaning-makers and meaning-sharers. As such, its importance for business and management research is self-evident. The organizations for whom we work, with which we collaborate or compete, or which otherwise touch our daily lives, cannot help but be concerned with the meanings made and shared within and about them. They need, for example, to understand their competitors' perspectives on the market in which they operate, to manage their staff successfully through rapid technological change, to help professionals from disparate disciplines to work effectively together, to communicate their brand image in a positive way to the public. Qualitative research is ideally placed to help organizations answer questions like these - and many others besides. In so doing, qualitative researchers typically collect large amounts of detailed textual data, from interviews, observations, online sources, organizational documents and the like. (Increasingly, written textual data are supplemented by visual data too.) And this is where such research faces its greatest challenge; how to make sense of the data in a way that holds on to its richness but does not drown in its sheer volume.

The fact that you are reading this book suggests that you are considering the use of Template Analysis as a way to face this challenge in your Master's dissertation research. You may be at an early stage of planning a qualitative project and trying to work out how to frame your research question(s) and design your study incorporating Template Analysis. Or perhaps you already have a stack of interview transcripts and are wondering how you turn these into a few thousand words of findings in your dissertation. It's always better if you choose your analytical method from the start, but even if you rushed to collect data without properly thinking through how you would analyse it, there's no need to panic! Our aim in this book is to introduce you to Template Analysis in a way that will enable you to do a thorough and professional job of data analysis in your own research. We will explain how it relates to other forms of analysis in its procedures and philosophical position, and take you through all the steps in the process of carrying out Template Analysis. We will provide numerous examples of studies in different organizational settings that have used the approach, including two detailed case examples from our own research. Finally, we will consider the overall strengths and limitations of Template Analysis, helping you to make a persuasive case for the method you have chosen and the way that you have used it.

Turning to the present chapter, our aims here are to briefly explain to you what Template Analysis is, and clarify how it is located within the wider field of thematic analysis. We will then provide you with an overview of the kinds of research designs, settings and topics within business and management research where Template Analysis may successfully be utilized.

OVERVIEW OF TEMPLATE ANALYSIS

History of Template Analysis

As far back as the early 1950s, Kracauer (1952) was arguing for a distinctly qualitative form of content analysis, against quantitative approaches that in his words confounded meaningful text 'with dead matter'. In the ensuing decades, qualitative researchers have developed a wide range of different ways to analyse textual data in a manner that focuses on human experience and meaning-making. Many of these can be characterized as 'thematic' approaches that seek to identify distinctive themes within a data set which shed light on important features of the topic under study. As we discuss below, sometimes such methods are incorporated into a wider methodology such as Grounded Theory (Glaser and Strauss, 1967) or Interpretative Phenomenological Analysis (IPA) (Smith et al., 2009). On other occasions, authors have proposed generic forms of thematic analysis that do not come with particular methodological commitments (e.g. Miles and Huberman, 1994; Braun and Clarke, 2006).

Template Analysis evolved as a generic approach within the wider tradition of thematic analysis, specifically among approaches with a strong emphasis on research in real-world settings. Our first encounter with it was in Crabtree and Miller's book *Doing Qualitative Research* (1992) which in this first edition was part of a series on Research Methods for Primary Care. At this point, Nigel was working on a qualitative project looking at general practitioners' decision-making regarding whether to refer patients to hospital – the 'template style' described by Crabtree and Miller (1992) appeared well suited to the pragmatic requirements of the project (see King et al., 1994, for more detail of how Template Analysis was used in this study). Nigel continued to use the technique in subsequent studies and contributed chapters on it to a series of books edited by Catherine Cassell and Gillian Symon (King, 1998, 2004, 2012). He also developed a website on the technique which has been very widely used (www.hud.ac.uk/hhs/research/template-analysis/) as well as more recently a Facebook page (www.facebook.com/TemplateAnalysis). Jo joined Nigel's Research Centre in 2009 and became actively involved in the use and development of Template Analysis, for example in two projects on chronic pain and work participation (Brooks et al., 2013; McCluskey et al., 2011) that form the basis for one of the case examples in Chapter 4 of this book.

Outline of Template Analysis procedures

As a form of qualitative data analysis, Template Analysis seeks to balance flexibility and structure in how it handles textual data. More specifically, we characterize it as a style of thematic analysis, as we discuss later in this chapter. Template Analysis can be described as a process typically undertaken in a sequence of seven steps, which we outline below. These are explained much more fully in Chapter 3.

1. *Familiarization with the data*. Before you begin any systematic analysis, it is always important to become as familiar as you can with your data. The better you know your data, the more able you will be to carry out a high-quality analysis. You should read through transcripts (or other items of textual data) several times before you begin any further work on the data. Where you have used audio-recordings of interviews (individual or group), or collected audio-diary accounts, you might find it helpful to listen to the recordings as well.
2. *Preliminary coding*. At this stage you note anything in your data that might be relevant to answering your research question(s). As well as highlighting points of interest that strike you as you read the data, you may also look out for material that supports *a priori* themes; that is, themes tentatively defined in advance based on theoretical or pragmatic interests related to your study. Preliminary coding in Template Analysis is typically carried out on a subset of the data. To give a hypothetical example, you might code the first three of ten interviews at this stage.
3. *Clustering*. On the basis of the preliminary analysis, emerging and *a priori* themes are clustered into meaningful groups and ordered hierarchically, with broader themes encompassing one or more levels of more narrowly focused themes.
4. *Producing an initial template*. The clusters of themes serve as the basis for producing an initial version of your coding template. You represent the template with a diagram showing the hierarchical organization of themes within each cluster, and sometimes including links across clusters.

5. *Developing the template*. The initial template is then applied to further data items (transcripts, field notes, diary entries, and so on). The template is amended where weaknesses are found in how well it captures what is relevant and potentially important in the data, and applied and modified in an iterative fashion.
6. *Applying the final template*. Once no more significant changes are needed to ensure that all data of relevance can be covered, the full data set is coded to the final version of the template. The analyst then uses the template to help them develop their interpretation of the data.
7. *Writing up*. The final template is used to help you organize the way you present your analysis in your dissertation.

LOCATING TEMPLATE ANALYSIS WITHIN QUALITATIVE DATA ANALYSIS

We are sometimes asked by students whether they should use Template Analysis or thematic analysis for their study. In response, we try as politely as possible to point out that this is a false choice. It is rather like someone asking their friend whether they would prefer 'a cat or a mammal' as a pet; in both cases the former is a subset of the latter, not an alternative to it. The fault is generally not that of the student but rather of methodological writers and teachers who present one particular form of thematic analysis as if it defined the whole approach. We therefore feel it is very important to be clear about how we see the relationship between Template Analysis and thematic analysis, and indeed thematic analysis and qualitative data analysis more widely.

Thematic analysis refers to a broad approach to organizing and interpreting qualitative data, within which many different styles or forms exists (including Template Analysis). All styles of thematic analysis include two inter-related core processes: *defining themes* that characterize significant features of the data, and *organizing* them in some kind of structure that represents conceptual relationships between the themes. Differences between styles of thematic analysis are the product of differences in how themes are defined and/or how the structures are arranged. Theoretical and philosophical differences in methodologies using thematic analysis can also influence the style of analysis, as well as its content. Note that not all forms of qualitative textual analysis are thematic; discourse and conversation analysis (Wetherell et al., 2001) do not involve defining and organizing themes, nor do those phenomenological approaches that seek to identify 'essences' of phenomena from accounts of experience through a process of condensing or distilling (Moustakas, 1994; Giorgi and Giorgi, 2008). However, there can be little doubt that thematic analysis remains the most widely used form of analysis across qualitative research as a whole.

KEY FEATURES OF THEMATIC ANALYSIS - AND HOW TEMPLATE ANALYSIS RELATES TO THEM

There are many ways in which styles of thematic analysis can be categorized. We have chosen to concentrate on three that we think are helpful in making higher-level distinctions between styles, and thus useful for researchers who need to decide which style would best suit their needs. Note that we are not talking here about distinctions in the fine detail of how coding is carried out. Saldaña (2009) identifies 28 different coding methods, but makes the point that these are not mutually exclusive; analysis styles are likely to employ several of these methods across stages of their procedures. Our focus here is on features that characterize styles as a whole, namely: *methodology-specific vs generic*, the *induction–deduction balance*, and their typical approach to *building the coding structure*. We will examine each of these in turn and consider how Template Analysis is positioned in relation to them.

Methodology-specific vs generic approaches

As we noted earlier, thematic analysis is sometimes used as an integral part of a distinct methodology. Well-known examples include Grounded Theory in its various forms (e.g. Charmaz, 2014; Corbin and Strauss, 2015) and Interpretative Phenomenological Analysis (IPA) (Smith et al., 2009). In such cases, while the thematic analysis procedures may be similar to those utilised in other approaches, they are used from a particular philosophical position that shapes the nature of the coding undertaken. Thus, Grounded Theory seeks to uncover and theorize social processes relating to a particular setting (a community, social group, organization, etc.), while IPA seeks to provide an understanding of a phenomenon as experienced in the everyday lives of participants (e.g. Tomkins and Eatough's (2014) study of how people managed their co-existent roles as employees and carers). It is therefore unjustifiable to collect your data and then afterwards declare that you are analysing it using Grounded Theory or IPA (or any other specific methodology). You need to 'buy in' to the methodology as a whole from the start, as it will guide you in how you should sample participants, collect data, present findings and draw conclusions - not just how you analyse the data.

Generic styles of thematic analysis are not wedded to any one methodological approach and underlying philosophy. Rather, they describe ways of carrying out analysis that you as a researcher need to tailor to the position your research is taking. Template Analysis is a generic style, as it does not insist on any particular philosophical or theoretical commitments on the part of the researcher. Other examples include Matrix Analysis (Nadin and Cassell, 2004), Framework Analysis (Ritchie and Spencer, 1994), Analytic Induction (Johnson, 2004) and various versions of qualitative content analysis (Hsieh and Shannon, 2005).

The requirement when using a generic style to work out for yourself how you will position it methodologically and philosophically allows you to ensure your analysis is driven by the specific needs of your study; it avoids the danger of taking a whole methodology 'off the shelf' and applying it in something of a rote fashion, without responding to the particularities of your aims and setting. Conversely, there is a danger with generic styles that they are used without any explicit concern for philosophical and methodological positions, often resulting in rather flat and superficial analyses. We discuss philosophical issues – especially as they relate to Template Analysis – in more detail in Chapter 2.

The induction–deduction balance

Forms of thematic analysis vary in the extent to which they use inductive or deductive forms of reasoning. Inductive reasoning is concerned with moving from specific observations to more general propositions about the topic under study. In contrast, deductive reasoning starts with abstract and generalized theory from which hypotheses are derived, to be tested against the data. Overall, inductive reasoning is more typical of qualitative research, while deductive reasoning is more typical of quantitative – through surveys, randomized controlled trials and experiments, for instance. In reality though, relatively few methods of qualitative data analysis are purely inductive, and we can look at thematic approaches in terms of where they strike the balance between induction and deduction. Grounded Theory and IPA are highly inductive, as is Analytic Induction. More deductive approaches to qualitative analysis tend to be those which are strongly theory-led and/or where coding categories or themes are largely defined in advance (e.g. Hayes, 1997; Kiffin-Petersen et al., 2012). Template Analysis does not have a single fixed position in the induction–deduction balance; this will vary according to the kind of methodological approach within which it is being used (see contrasting examples in Chapter 5, for example). However, it is fair to say that it is usually neither at the most strongly inductive nor most strongly deductive ends, and can therefore be seen as tending to occupy the mid-range of this continuum.

Building the coding structure

Many forms of thematic analysis suggest a rather fixed sequence by which the researcher builds up their coding structure in the analysis process. Often this is aimed at ensuring the data analyst remains close to the text at the start and avoids developing more abstract and interpretive themes too soon. This is true of the generic style of thematic analysis presented by Braun and Clark (2006) as well as the way thematic analysis is used in the specific methodologies of IPA (Smith et al., 2009) and Grounded Theory (Charmaz, 2014; Corbin and Strauss, 2015). In contrast, Template Analysis is more flexible in the sequence by which the coding structure (template) is built up, and does not insist that more 'interpretive' forms of coding are only used after a 'descriptive' stage. In addition, Template Analysis tends to encourage greater depth of coding than many other thematic approaches – where data are rich and highly relevant to the research question, a researcher may code to four or more levels to elaborate fine distinctions within main themes.

LOCATING TEMPLATE ANALYSIS WITHIN BUSINESS AND MANAGEMENT RESEARCH

Having introduced you to Template Analysis as a style of thematic analysis, in this section we will give you an overview of how this approach has been utilized within business and management research. We will consider the types of data that may be analysed using Template Analysis and the types of research design into which it may be incorporated. Finally, we will describe the wide range of topic areas that business and management researchers have addressed using Template Analysis.

Types of data

Template Analysis is an approach that can be used with any kind of textual data – that is, data in the form of written words. Interviews are the most commonly used method of data collection in qualitative research as a whole (King and Horrocks, 2010), so it is not surprising that they are also by some way the most common source of data analysed by Template Analysis. Because Template Analysis emphasizes the importance of being able to go back to the data to support the themes you construct and organize, it is normal for the approach to utilize full verbatim transcripts of interviews. This means transcripts where every word spoken by the interviewee (and the interviewer) is recorded in written form, alongside other features of communication that might help convey meaning – for example, you might note long pauses before answering questions, an ironic, angry or otherwise emotional tone of voice, and so on (for more on transcription, see Poland, 2002; King and Horrocks, 2010). Template Analysis does not require the kind of fine detail in transcription used in methods like conversation analysis (Jefferson, 1984) where word-by-word changes in intonation are signalled, pauses and overlaps timed to the second, and so on. Extensive summaries could be used for analysis rather than full transcripts, but this would inevitably create extra distance between research participants' own accounts of their experiences and your analytical judgements about them. Such a strategy would be most defensible where you had an especially large volume of data to manage or where a 'quick and dirty' snapshot analysis was needed in a very short time span. On the whole it is unlikely to be a good choice for a higher-level undergraduate, Master's or doctoral research project.

The face-to-face individual interview, using a semi-structured format, can be seen as the standard approach in qualitative business and management research, as in many other disciplines. In this the researcher comes prepared with a topic guide highlighting areas they wish to cover, but this is used flexibly with plenty of opportunity for the interviewee to lead the conversation in directions that are important to them. However, there are many other forms of interview, each presenting its own challenges for data analysis. One major form that you will often see in the business and management literature is the group interview (Kandola, 2012). When using Template Analysis with group interview data, make sure that you index which member of a group is making which comments. If you fail to do that, you can end up presenting a particular theme as being prominent for the group as a whole when in fact it might just be the idiosyncratic concern of one member. Tomkins and Eatough (2010) present a useful example of how individual contributions can be tracked within focus group data, in a study of the experience of being a working carer. Another key issue in analysing group interview data is that you should seek to capture the nature of the interaction among members, not simply the topic content of what they say. You may well find it helpful to develop themes within Template Analysis that explicitly address this; for instance, you might have a thematic cluster named 'group atmosphere' with sub-themes like 'hostility', 'friendliness' and 'guardedness'.

Another form of interview that is increasingly popular is the online interview. These are of two main types that differ rather significantly. Synchronous online interviews are conducted in real time using 'chat' facilities or services such as Skype and FaceTime (the latter two of course allow for video as well as audio communication). Asynchronous online interviews are generally conducted via e-mail and consist of an exchange of questions and answers between interviewer and interviewee over a period of days, weeks or even months. With regard to the requirements for analysis, it is the latter type that need to be treated rather differently from face-to-face interviews. In asynchronous online interviews, the interviewee has the chance to reflect for a considerable time period on his or her answers, and also can easily refer back to how they answered previous questions. It may therefore be important in coding and template development to be sure that the temporal sequence of interviewee responses is recognized. For instance, as a result of extended reflection on their position, a participant may come to a new perspective on a topic, and you may want to represent this explicitly in your coding.

Although interview methods remain prominent, there are many other forms of data collection you will come across in qualitative business and management research, which can readily be analysed using Template Analysis. If you are at the planning stage of your project, it is certainly worthwhile to think about alternatives to interviews which could suit your needs better. One option is to ask participants to provide their own written accounts of their experiences in relation to the subject of your research. There are two main ways in which this kind of data may be collected: participant diaries and qualitative questionnaires. E-mail interviews can also be seen as a version of this, but they retain an interactive element that is absent in these other methods. Diary methods require participants to keep a regular record of their experiences relating to the research topic over a set period of time. The extent of structure provided by researchers varies, depending on the overall research approach and design. For instance, Hughes et al. (2010) collected quite structured diary data from 35 doctors about their use of online information during their working day. Radcliffe (2013) used a more loosely structured diary in her study of work–life decision-making. Quite often, a diary method is supplemented with one or more interviews with diary participants (or a subset of them). Waddington (2005) supplemented diaries with telephone interviews in her study of gossip and emotion in nursing, as did Poppleton et al. (2008) in their investigation of work–non-work relationships among blue- and white-collar workers. A clear strength of diaries is that they capture experience over time. They also do not necessitate the very time-consuming process of audio-transcription, though if hand-written rather than typed legibility can be a problem.

Qualitative questionnaires are paper or online questionnaires where the great majority of questions are open-ended, eliciting detailed textual answers. They enable the researcher to collect textual data from relatively large numbers of participants, and/or from people who would be difficult to access face-to-face. As with diaries, they do not require audio-transcription. These potential advantages are at the cost of depth of response compared to interviews and the more extensive versions of the diary method. A good example of Template Analysis used with qualitative questionnaire data is Kidd's (2008) study of the components of career well-being. She used an online questionnaire (n = 89) with two broad questions asking for accounts of an occasion in their working life when her participants felt respectively positive and negative about their careers, and their feelings and emotions at these times. The use of two main questions of a very open-ended nature was in keeping with Kidd's exploratory approach, and was also reflected in the 'bottom-up' way in which she used Template Analysis (for example, not defining any a priori themes).

Another type of data with which Template Analysis may be used is observational field notes. Qualitative observational studies vary in the extent to which the researchers are actively engaged in the social setting which they are studying: from pure observer roles where there is minimal interaction with those observed, to full participant observation in which they actively take part in everyday organizational life (Brannan and Oultram, 2012). It is common for observational methods to be used alongside interviews (and sometimes other methods such as documentary analysis), as the diverse forms of data collection produce different but complementary understandings of participants' experiences. In such designs, a coding template may be developed on the basis of the interview data first, and then applied to the observational field notes later in the analytic process – as illustrated in Frambach et al.'s (2014) study of problem-based learning in medical schools. Alternately, the data from all the methods of collection may be pooled and all fed into the analysis from the start, as in the case of Wang and Bowie's (2009) study of revenue management and its impact on business-to-business relationships.

A further source of data that can and has been analysed using Template Analysis is pre-existing organizational documents. These take many forms: minutes of meetings, policy and procedural documents, internal and external reports, marketing material, and so on. There are also documents about organizations: newspaper and magazine articles, for instance. Clearly, the choice of which documents to select and what kind of research question to address with them is crucial, though these issues of research design are beyond the scope of the present book (see Lee (2012) for a good overview of the issues in this type of research). Studies using organizational documents vary so greatly in terms of the type and amount of material used, the theoretical and/or philosophical positions taken, and so on, that it is not possible to talk in any general terms about the challenges of using TA with documentary data. In fact, the flexibility inherent to TA means that it can be adapted to very varied document-based studies. For instance, Maguire (2008) analysed 13 US exercise manuals in a study of the relationship between leisure and obligations of 'self-work' in the fitness industry, while Maznevski and Chudoba (2000) analysed company documents such as minutes, reports and vision statements alongside interview and observational data in their examination of global virtual team dynamics and effectiveness.

As can be seen in some of the studies we have referred to above, it is common in qualitative business and management research for more than one form of data collection to be used. Sometimes the different forms of data are analysed using different methods, but if you wanted to use TA for the full data set you need to decide whether to use a single template for all the data, or to develop a separate template for each data set. The former strategy is more common, probably because it readily allows for integration of analysis across data types. The kind of circumstance in which you might choose to develop separate templates is when different data types are addressing clearly distinct aims and objectives within the overall project.

Types of study design

Template Analysis is not at all restricted in the type of study design within which it may be used. We will highlight here some of the main ways in which the choice of research design may influence how TA is used; this question is explored in much more detail in Chapters 4 and 5. Most qualitative studies in business and management are cross-sectional in design, in that they collect data from a sample of participants at one point in time (by interviews or some other method) and look for commonalities and differences among them. It is not surprising, therefore, that most published examples of the use of Template Analysis fit this mould too. One type of cross-sectional design that does raise particular analytical issues is where there is a strong emphasis on inter-group comparisons. For example, in one of our studies we looked at how different groups of community nurse (District Nurses and Community Matrons) understood their own and each other's roles in palliative care (King et al., 2010). In such studies, if you are using TA you face a decision as to whether to develop a single template for both groups – and then compare the pattern of themes across the groups – or develop separate templates and allow differences between these to help focus your comparison. There is no right or wrong choice here, but a key factor is likely to be whether there is a substantial degree of commonality in experiences and concerns across groups. If there is, then a single template may be the most efficient choice; if not, separate templates may make sense. In the community nurse study, we found a single template the best way to enable comparison between the groups. In contrast, in their study of the experiences of black and minority ethnic (BME) managers' careers, Wyatt and Silvester (2015) constructed different templates for BME and white managers.

Longitudinal studies are those that collect data from participants at a number of points over time, usually through repeat interviews, diaries, e-mail interviews (or a combination of methods). While there are a fair number of longitudinal studies that have used Template Analysis (e.g. Lips-Wiersma and Hall, 2007; Corsaro and Snehota, 2011) they tend to present an analysis of the data as a whole. We would like to see TA used to capture the temporal dimension of the data. This could be done by indexing all coding by the time point to which it relates, so the researcher can examine whether and how patterns of themes change over the course of the study.

Qualitative evaluation studies seek to examine the effectiveness of particular instances of organizational change, innovation or development, from the perspective of the experiences of those involved in or affected by them. They may be cross-sectional or longitudinal in design, and vary across the whole range of philosophical and methodological positions in research. Template Analysis can be a useful form of data analysis for qualitative evaluation studies, because of its flexible and pragmatic nature. In particular, the use of *a priori* themes allows you as a researcher to shape your analysis to the evaluation criteria of a particular project, while still allowing for unanticipated issues to be captured in emergent themes. For instance, in the qualitative part of a mixed methods evaluation of an innovative palliative care service, we used evaluation criteria relating to how the service worked with other stakeholders to inform *a priori* themes in our analysis (Brooks and King, 2014).

Finally, Template Analysis may be used for the qualitative part of mixed methods projects that involve a combination of quantitative and qualitative methods. An example is Kelliher and Anderson's (2010) study of flexible working practices. Again, the potential to use *a priori* themes can be helpful in facilitating qualitative analysis that can be integrated with the quantitative element. So, if the survey part of a mixed methods study draws on particular theoretical ideas, these can also feed into the qualitative analysis through the way *a priori* themes are formulated.

Research settings and topics

Template Analysis has been used in many areas of human and social scientific research, including health and social care, education, sport and exercise science as well as business and management. Equally, within business and management studies, both the organizational settings and the types of topics addressed in research using Template Analysis are extremely diverse. There are studies in large multinational corporations, health services, educational institutions, SMEs, the voluntary sector – indeed pretty much anywhere that business and management research takes place. Similarly, topics using Template Analysis are as diverse as disease-prevention decision-making by pig farmers (Alarcon et al., 2014), the impact of family-friendly policies on expatriate Pakistani employees (Khokher and Beauregard, 2014) and communities of practice in science-based SMEs (Pattinson and Preece, 2014). The remaining chapters in this book should help you think about how best to use Template Analysis for your own research.

OVERVIEW OF THIS BOOK

Now that we have introduced you to Template Analysis and its place in qualitative research in business and management, the rest of this book will explain and examine the method in more depth, to enable you to use it successfully in your own work. In Chapter 2 we will consider how philosophical issues in the research process relate to Template Analysis. Chapter 3 provides a detailed account of the steps involved in utilizing Template Analysis, expanding on the summary presented near the start of the current chapter. In Chapter 4 we move on to describe two contrasting examples of Masters level projects utilising Template Analysis. We then build on this to present a wider range of examples from the business and management research literature in Chapter 5. Finally, in Chapter 6 we evaluate the overall strengths and possible limitations of Template Analysis as a method for Master's students in business and management.

CHAPTER SUMMARY

Within this chapter we have:

- described the historical development of Template Analysis
- outlined its key procedural steps
- discussed the place of Template Analysis within qualitative data analysis more widely, and in particular considered how it relates to other thematic forms of analysis
- located Template Analysis within business and management research
- provided an overview of the rest of this book.

2

PHILOSOPHICAL ISSUES WHEN USING TEMPLATE ANALYSIS

INTRODUCTION

In Chapter 1, we introduced you to Template Analysis as a generic style of thematic analysis widely used in qualitative business and management research. As we pointed out, Template Analysis is not wedded to any one methodological approach or underlying philosophy. However, while Template Analysis does not insist on any particular specific philosophical or theoretical commitments on the part of the researcher, this does not render these commitments unimportant or inconsequential. It means, rather, that the onus is on you as a researcher to reflect on and elucidate your own particular philosophical position. In this chapter, we will introduce you to some of the main aspects of the philosophy of research of which you need to be aware, then consider the ways in which this impacts on how Template Analysis should (or should not) be used in your business and management research project.

UNDERSTANDING THE PHILOSOPHICAL POSITION OF RESEARCH

Template Analysis is a qualitative research method. *Method* refers to the particular techniques used to collect and analyse data in research. As we saw in Chapter 1, there is a wide range of methods of data collection in qualitative research, including interviews (one-to-one, focus groups, online), research diaries, participant observation and the use of pre-existing texts. Methods are informed by *methodology* – that is, the general approach taken to carrying out a piece of research. Different methodologies are shaped by different underlying philosophical and theoretical assumptions. Ideally, before undertaking any piece of qualitative research, you should first consider the philosophical position your work is coming from, as your philosophical stance has important implications for data collection and analysis.

In order to understand why it is necessary to think about your philosophical assumptions when undertaking qualitative research, there are some key terms with which you need to become familiar. *Epistemology* is the philosophical theory of knowledge, and refers to the assumptions we make about *what* it is possible for us to know and *how* we can obtain this knowledge. *Ontology* refers to philosophical assumptions about the nature of being, which determine what we can know to be real, and what we can know to exist. Understanding these terms may be difficult, and it might be tempting to dismiss them as florid, convoluted issues of no real-life or applied relevance for your own research. However, all research involves epistemological and ontological assumptions, whether or not these are explicitly addressed. These assumptions have very real and practical consequences for choices you make in terms of your research area, your research question, the data you collect, the analysis undertaken and the way in which you report your findings. This is of particular importance in qualitative research, as we shall explain now.

In qualitative research, the essential concern is with human beings as meaning-makers. Qualitative approaches, examining how the social world is experienced and understood, are generally founded upon *interpretivism*. Human experience is the central focus of research. Individuals' accounts of their experiences enable researchers to gain a better understanding of the social world they inhabit. This is rather different from other forms of traditional scientific research, which tends to be concerned with accurate measurement and prediction. The sociologist Max Weber (1864–1920) distinguished between the natural sciences and the human sciences, arguing that the latter should be concerned with *verstehen* (understanding) rather than *erklaren* (explanation). This commitment to *verstehen* is inherent in all interpretive research traditions, which prioritize the exploration of meaning over the establishment of causal relationships.

For those undertaking quantitative research in business and management, epistemology and ontology will often not be given any detailed or overt consideration. This is because such research often (tacitly) assumes that the phenomena under investigation exist independently, can be objectively observed from a neutral stance and can be accurately measured. Management and organizational research has often been characterized as being underpinned by *positivism* (Duberley et al., 2012). The positivist approach suggests the goal of research is to provide objective knowledge, and to develop general laws or principles to explain phenomena. However, although mainstream quantitative research is still often described as positivist, it is probably more accurate nowadays to describe it as *post-positivist*. *Post-positivism*, a term associated with the philosophy of Karl Popper (1902–1994), is an approach that advocates the principles of *hypothetico-deductivism* (we should come up with formal theories about the world which we can test) and *falsification* (we should then seek to disprove or falsify these theories or hypotheses).

Positivist and post-positivist approaches can be said to be taking a *realist* position in both epistemological and ontological terms. A realist approach subscribes to the view that there is a real-world or objective reality 'out there' that exists independently of us, and that we can have some kind of access to further knowledge about this world using appropriate methods and techniques. As we discuss below, there is variation among realist approaches in how they view such access to independent reality. An alternative to realism is a *relativist* stance. From this position, knowledge and reality are always open to a range of interpretations, relative to our historical, cultural and social contexts. Notions of 'real' and 'true' are rather different from this perspective. For example, some researchers take the view that it is impossible to neutrally observe the social world because we are inevitably influencing what we see through the act of observation. Equally, our interpretations cannot be entirely detached from our own position in the world and our methodological choices. From this standpoint, the idea that there is objective knowledge about an independently existing world waiting to be uncovered through appropriate measurement is not supportable.

However, portraying the ontological perspectives available to researchers as either realist or relativist is a little crude – the options are really more nuanced than this simplistic distinction suggests. Similarly, qualitative and quantitative researchers need not be portrayed as necessarily diametrically opposed – what is important to point out is that they might need to take different approaches based on different understandings of what they can and what they might like to research. King and Horrocks (2010) use the example of different understandings of human behaviour to demonstrate how a topic can be explored in quite diverse ways from different perspectives. If a researcher believes that behaviour is mainly determined by genetic inheritance, their epistemological and ontological position (as well as their choice of an appropriate way to research or investigate behaviour) will be rather different from that of a researcher who assumes that people's behaviour is brought about by their interactions in social situations. *Critical realism* is an example of an alternative perspective that acknowledges the social construction of reality, but retains a core element of ontological realism, arguing that there are realities which exist independent of human activity. From this perspective, for example, while structures outside an individual's control (e.g. biological, social or economic) may not directly determine behaviour, they are nonetheless recognized as having important influences in understanding experience.

IDENTIFYING A PHILOSOPHICAL POSITION IN STUDIES USING TEMPLATE ANALYSIS

So, we have seen how the choice of a method of data analysis for a piece of qualitative research needs to be guided by its methodological position and the underlying epistemological and ontological assumptions. As we discussed in Chapter 1, there are some qualitative data analysis methods which are directly linked to particular methodologies (for example, Interpretative Phenomenological Analysis, which is, as the name suggests, linked to a phenomenological approach; Discourse Analysis methods with social constructionist approaches – these positions will be explained more fully shortly). Template Analysis, in contrast, is not a distinct methodology but rather a style of analysis, and can therefore be used in qualitative research from a range of philosophical positions. This ability to use Template Analysis flexibly within different philosophical approaches may be seen as an advantage of the method. However, with a generic method like Template Analysis, the onus is on those utilizing it to be explicit and upfront about the position they are adopting in their work. Writers on qualitative methods have suggested a variety of ways of distinguishing the different philosophical positions taken within the field. For example, Reicher (2000) divides qualitative methods into 'experiential' and 'discursive' approaches. Madill et al. (2000) classify methods as 'realist', 'contextual constructionist' and 'radical constructionist', while also recognizing there are important distinctions within these broad positions. The emphasis in these classifications is on epistemology – what claims different methods make as to what our data enable us to know about the world. This question does tend to be at the forefront of researcher's minds when thinking about how they plan to use Template Analysis, but we would argue that it is important not to neglect ontological considerations – what claims you want to make about the nature of reality. Sometimes, methodological approaches that on the face of it have rather similar epistemological positions differ with regard to ontology, with significant consequences for aspects of research practice. We will describe below four different philosophical positions within which Template Analysis may be used: *qualitative neo-positivist, limited realist, contextualist* and *radical constructionist*. We will highlight how the epistemological and ontological claims of these positions impact on good practice in the use of Template Analysis. Table 2.1 summarizes the distinctive features of each of these four positions, and their main implications for Template Analysis.

Qualitative neo-positivism

We borrow this term from Duberley et al. (2012), to refer to qualitative research which is undertaken from a realist position not unlike the conventional positivistic stance taken in mainstream quantitative research. Work in this tradition is sometimes referred to rather dismissively as 'naïve realist'; we prefer Duberley et al.'s term

Table 2.1 Different philosophical positions for research and their implications for the use of Template Analysis

Philosophical position	Ontology	Epistemology	Implications for use of Template Analysis
Neo-positivism	Realist	Realist	Emphasis on minimizing impact of researcher subjectivity Use of independent coders May use strong, theory-linked *a priori* themes
Limited realism	Realist	Constructivist/Relativist	Often uses *a priori* themes informed by theory or evaluation criteria Quality checks to stimulate critical thinking, specific to needs of particular study Reflexivity in analysis important, to go beyond researcher subjectivity
Contextualism	Relativist (or indeterminate)	Constructivist/Relativist	Loose, highly tentative use of *a priori* themes (if at all) Reflexivity: researcher subjectivity integral to whole process
Radical constructionism	Relativist	Strongly relativist	Scepticism about any quality criteria in analysis Focus on themes as aspects of discursive construction rather than of direct experience

because it allows that researchers may have a clear rationale for adopting such an approach, rather than simply exhibiting naïvety. We distinguish it from the more limited forms of realism that are variously labelled 'critical realism', 'subtle realism' and 'perspectival realism' among other terms. These are covered in the next section.

Research adopting a qualitative neo-positivist position takes the view that individuals are part of an observable and knowable world, and that there is a relatively unproblematic relationship between our view of the world, and the real, material world 'out there'. It assumes that research participants' accounts directly represent this reality, and that as researchers we can take steps to remove subjective bias from our investigations. This position is thus strongly realist in both its ontology (beliefs about the nature of reality) and epistemology (beliefs regarding what we can know about reality). Researchers may decide to take such a position where their research is strongly tied to existing theory, including in mixed methods studies where it offers the advantage of philosophical congruity between the quantitative and qualitative arms of a project (e.g. Hughes et al., 2010).

If using Template Analysis from a qualitative neo-positive position, you will need to show a concern for minimizing the impact of researcher subjectivity. Using independent coders would be recommended; these could be fellow student researchers or experts in your methodology and/or topic area. (We discuss details of these kinds of quality check in Chapter 3.) This is the only one of our four philosophical positions in which the use of statistical inter-rater reliability calculations might be justifiable and useful – though not compulsory. In addition to these implications for quality checks, using Template Analysis from this perspective would necessitate a clear, consistent use of the steps in the analysis process, with less scope for adaptation and flexibility than other positions. This is because you would need to demonstrate consistency in procedures for the whole of your data to enhance claims for objectivity. Finally, you are likely to choose a neo-positive approach to Template Analysis if you want to work within a strong existing theoretical framework, so you would be likely to use well-defined, theoretically driven *a priori* themes in your analysis. Maznevski and Chudoba (2000), for instance, used *a priori* themes informed by Adaptive Structuration Theory in a mixed methods study of global virtual team dynamics.

Limited realist

We use the term 'limited realism' here to refer to a range of related philosophical positions that call themselves such things as 'critical realism' (Archer et al., 1998), 'subtle realism' (Hammersley, 1992) and 'natural realism' (Putnam, 1999), among others (see Maxwell (2012) for further discussion). What all these positions have in common is a commitment to a realist ontology combined with a constructivist epistemology. Put simply, they believe the world has a reality outside of human constructions of it, but that our understanding of it is always limited by our position within it. Intangible things such as mental phenomena, social forces and culture are just as 'real' as physical phenomena, and can influence our behaviour and experience. However, in contrast to the neo-positivist position described in the previous section, limited realists hold that we cannot ever remove our subjectivity from the analytical process.

Limited realist research is often concerned with producing causal explanations of social phenomena, and seeks some degree of generalizability – albeit a more cautious and nuanced form than in neo-positivist qualitative research. It also commonly draws on and seeks to develop theory (Maxwell, 2012). Thus, while limited realist qualitative research does not claim objectivity, it also rejects the position of more relativist and constructionist positions that no interpretation of data is 'better' than any other. When analysing data, the researcher needs to question his or her assumptions and seek to develop an interpretation that is as credible as possible; reflexivity is therefore an important part of the research process.

Given that the approaches we have covered under the heading 'limited realist' include quite a varied range of positions, there cannot be a single prescription for how such research should incorporate Template Analysis. However, there are some issues that you are likely to need to consider if you are taking such an approach. Firstly, limited realist work will often seek to draw on existing theory and/or develop theory in a specific area; the use of theoretically informed *a priori* themes is therefore quite common. An example is Shaw and Wainwright's (2007) study of Critical Success Factors (CSFs) in a healthcare IT system, which utilizes *a priori* themes derived from the existing CSF literature. Similarly, evaluation studies using a limited realist approach may well employ *a priori* themes related to evaluation criteria and/or theory underpinning the evaluation. Secondly, because limited realist studies on the one hand recognize the inevitable subjectivity of the researcher but on the other hand seek to develop understandings that are not simply a product of that subjectivity, reflexivity in the analysis process is important. Thirdly, limited realist researchers would not tend to use the kind of quality criteria employed in neo-positivist research, nor the technical checks such as the calculation of inter-rater reliability scores. Independent rating might well be used but more as a way to encourage critical thinking and reflection on unrecognized assumptions than to establish a particular interpretation as 'correct' (e.g. Dries and Pepermans, 2008). Indeed, Maxwell (2012) argues that critical realist research (using this as a broad term equivalent to our 'limited realist') should not rely on standardized quality checks based just on particular elements of methods; rather researchers need to think about threats to quality of interpretation in their particular study and consider their overall strategy for addressing these.

Contextualist

Qualitative research undertaken from a contextual position assumes that context – in historical, cultural and social terms – is integral to understanding how people experience and understand their lives. For researchers taking this position, all knowledge that can be obtained through research is always conditional and context specific. There is no single reality 'out there' which can be measured and objectively investigated. Both researcher and research participant are seen as conscious beings who are always interpreting and acting on and in the world, and all accounts that can be obtained through qualitative inquiry are therefore subjective. Notions of knowledge as being universal and value free are not sustainable from this perspective and given this, it is neither meaningful nor appropriate to try to impose or measure objectivity or reliability. However, those taking a contextual approach do understand their data as being part of a broader existence – that is, they seek to achieve some kind of grounding in participants' experiences and their social context for their results. Contextualist research may therefore be seen as taking a constructivist stance towards both ontology and epistemology. However, the form of constructivist epistemology it proposes is less strongly relativist than the radical constructionist position we describe below. The constructivist form of Grounded Theory (Charmaz, 2014), phenomenology (Langdridge, 2007), some readings of Personal Construct Psychology (Butt and Burr, 2004) and some forms of narrative analysis (McAdams, 1993) would normally be seen as occupying a contextualist position.

The specific contextualist approach within which Template Analysis is most commonly used is phenomenology. Developing from foundations in the philosophy of Husserl, Heidegger and Merleau-Ponty (Langdridge, 2007), phenomenological research is concerned with describing and making sense of people's first-hand experiences of particular aspects of their world. It takes the view that neither researcher nor participant has direct access to 'reality', but that we can nonetheless meaningfully analyse subjective experiences of the world. A researcher using Template Analysis from this perspective would assume that experience is real to the experiencer and that we can make sense of reported experience, while avoiding claims about what 'actually' happened. Note that phenomenological research is a broad church, and some phenomenologists argue for a position that is closer to limited realism (Finlay, 2009). This highlights the fact that the divisions between the philosophical positions we outline in this chapter are blurred – this needs to be borne in mind when you are thinking through the position of your particular study.

From a contextualist stance, then, there are always multiple interpretations to be made of any phenomena, and these interpretations will depend upon both the specific social context of the research and the position of the researcher. Researchers using Template Analysis from a contextualist stance will be likely to take a 'bottom up' approach to data analysis, using a priori themes cautiously, if at all. However, given that researcher subjectivity is acknowledged as integral (the researcher is seen not as a potential source of bias but as playing an active role in data generation and data analysis), a priori themes can be a useful way for a researcher to be explicitly upfront with regards to his or her own perspective on the research. A priori themes should always be seen as tentative and subject to removal if they do not work well with the data obtained – this may be particularly important to keep in mind when using Template Analysis from a contextualist stance. Template Analysis studies undertaken from this philosophical position will need to use the technique in a flexible way, considering multiple interpretations of the data, rather than one 'correct' reading.

As we have discussed, researcher subjectivity is integral to this sort of research and this is accepted and welcomed rather than seen as a source of bias. While recognizing that it is inevitable that one's own perspective is brought to research, it is argued that common cultural understandings and the empathy engendered through the recognition of a shared humanity are both important and valuable. As the researcher is recognized as active in both data generation and data analysis, one would expect to see researchers using Template Analysis from this epistemological position making an effort to communicate their own perspective – both to assist the reader in fully understanding their findings, and also to help the researcher recognize and move beyond their everyday assumptions. When using Template Analysis from a contextualist stance, one would therefore expect to see significant attention paid to researcher reflexivity. Questions that might need addressing may include, 'What was the nature of my involvement as a researcher in the research process?' and 'How did my involvement shape the outcomes of the research?' You should think about how your own assumptions about the research topic might, for instance, influence the way you formulate your research question, or the issues you highlight in your interview topic guide. Reflexivity needs to be both personal and methodological (Finlay, 2003). Personal reflexivity means thinking about the effect of your own position on the research process; for instance, do you have strong views or expectations with regard to the research topic? Methodological reflexivity means thinking about the impact of the methodological choices you have made; for instance, using focus groups rather than individual interviews.

Reflexivity should not be seen as something to be 'dealt with' only at certain points; attention should be paid to your own role in research throughout the research process. Nonetheless, it is possible to suggest a number of ways to attend to reflexivity in contextualist work using Template Analysis. Independent coding can be used as a way to highlight or challenge your assumptions, much as we suggested in relation to a limited realist approach. You can also use an audit trail as a means of making transparent the analytical choices you make in the course of data analysis. An audit trail consists of a documentary record of the steps undertaken and decisions made in moving from the raw data to a final interpretation of that data. Keeping an audit trail forces you to be explicit about the decisions you are making and to reflect upon how they led you on a course towards your findings and conclusions. Because of the focus on iterative development of the template, it is a good idea to keep successive versions of your template, ideally with some commentary to remind you at the end of the study of the thinking behind the way you developed it. These might be incorporated within a 'research journal', where you record your thoughts and feelings about doing the analysis.

Findings produced in a piece of research using Template Analysis from a contextualist stance may be very context specific as it is acknowledged that the knowledge that can be produced in such work does not claim to be universal. From a contextualist stance, it is acknowledged that there will be multiple possible interpretations to be made of any phenomena, and these will depend upon the position of the researcher, and the specific social context of the research. Such an approach will acknowledge and focus on the multiplicity of the potential perspectives available. From a contextualist position, it is important that the research participant's perspective is reflected on and explored, just as the researcher's role should be considered through the processes to promote researcher reflexivity previously suggested.

Radical constructionist

Radical constructionist approaches share a number of similarities with the contextualist position we have just covered, and many of the points we have made in relation to using Template Analysis from a contextualist approach would therefore also be applicable here. Constructionist approaches also take the view that avoiding 'bias' is meaningless, that knowledge is co-produced between researcher and research participant. Knowledge is also seen as being historically and culturally located. However, while contextual approaches maintain that research findings can be 'grounded' in participants' accounts, constructionism presents a challenge to the notion that there are any absolute foundations for knowledge at all. According to constructionists, 'reality' is socially and culturally produced and is constructed through language, especially in social interaction.

Radical constructionist approaches have an unambiguously relativist epistemology with a very strong emphasis on the role of language. To the extent that they concern themselves with ontology at all, radical constructionists clearly take a relativist view of it too. However, as Maxwell (2012) argues, many constructionist scholars simply see ontology and epistemology as reflections of each other; if all knowledge is constructed through language in interaction, then it follows that we cannot consider a reality that exists outside our constructions of it. The aim of research from this position is to explore how people construct versions of their world, and what resources they draw on to do so. It is often also concerned with how society limits the ways in which people may construct their world through the power of dominant discourses. Language is not seen as *representing* reality, instead language is assumed to *create* reality. Language is seen as productive and actively doing something: rather than there being one reality 'out there' which we can observe and measure, different versions of reality can be produced with different discourses.

Like the contextualist position, radical constructionism recognizes the researcher's active engagement in the production of knowledge, and the central importance of the social world(s) they inhabit. However, while the notion of objective truth is problematic for contextualism, constructivism goes further still, arguing that concepts of key importance for contextualists such as subjectivity and even the notion of knowledge itself are discursive devices or constructions. Constructivism is interested in the ways in which claims of knowledge are legitimated and how they function.

The applicability of Template Analysis to research taking a radical constructionist approach is more questionable than its application in work coming from other phenomenological positions. The approach is not suitable to use with constructionist methodologies concerned with the fine detail of how language constructs social reality in interaction, such as various types of discourse analysis (Arribas-Ayllon and Walkerdine, 2008; Potter, 2012; Gee, 2014), as these do not use thematic forms of analysis. However, there are examples of research which can be identified as working within a constructionist epistemology where text is looked at in a broader manner (e.g. Taylor and Ussher, 2001). This type of work, concerned with patterns of discourse use rather than close analysis of interactions, could certainly consider using Template Analysis although it would be crucial to be clear that themes elicited were defined in terms of aspects of discourse rather than personal experience.

The quality criteria applied to work undertaken from within a constructionist epistemology differ greatly from those that might be appropriate for work undertaken from a realist stance – notions of objectivity, validity and reliability are clearly unsuitable. Even alternative quality criteria such as 'credibility' and 'transferability' developed specifically for qualitative research (Lincoln and Guba, 1985) are seen as constructions that serve a rhetorical function. Researcher reflexivity, as described above in relation to contextualism, is again important and relevant, for its ability to enrich an account of how particular researchers produced knowledge in a particular setting. Other quality criteria might include audience appeal (do the findings contribute to understanding, do they facilitate productive action?) and ability of the findings to explain exceptions to the general rule as well as more typical examples (Madill et al., 2000). A further potential criterion is that of 'internal coherence'. The production of a logical, coherent and persuasive account is often proffered as a credible way by which to judge the success or otherwise of qualitative research generally. However, Madill and colleagues point out that as research of this type often focuses on questioning the extent to which any text is truly coherent or consistent, it is somewhat problematic to then apply criteria of coherence or consistency to the account of the research. They suggest the alternative criterion of 'no *abhorrent* contradictions' as a pragmatic alternative.

CHAPTER SUMMARY

In this chapter we have:

- explained why it is important to consider your philosophical position in qualitative research generally, and when using Template Analysis specifically
- considered four particular approaches – qualitative neo-positivist, limited realist, contextualist and radical constructionist – and described their ontological and epistemological positions
- discussed some of the main implications for the use of Template Analysis within each of these approaches
- emphasized that the boundaries between these approaches are fuzzy rather than clear-cut.

3

DOING TEMPLATE ANALYSIS: A GUIDE TO THE MAIN COMPONENTS AND PROCEDURES

In this chapter, we are going to lead you through the main procedural steps you will follow when undertaking Template Analysis. It is important to be clear from the start however that, while it is a systematic approach to coding qualitative data, Template Analysis is also a flexible technique that researchers can (and should) adapt to the needs of their particular study. This means that although there are certain generic steps to the technique which are applicable to any project, you should not view our description of the technique as narrowly prescriptive. As we saw in Chapter 2, it is always important in qualitative research to be explicit about how and why you have chosen to undertake your work in the way you have, so you can be sure there is consistency throughout the research process. Similarly, when using Template Analysis, you should be clear about why you have used it in a particular way and be able to justify your choices. Fortunately, because Template Analysis offers a structured approach to data coding, it lends itself well to providing an audit trail which allows for the clear demonstration and explanation of how you developed your themes and arrived at your final thematic structure. This can be helpful in establishing the quality of your final analysis through providing a means of recounting and explaining the decisions you made throughout the coding process.

Template Analysis emphasizes the use of hierarchical coding and central to the technique is the development of a *coding template*, usually on the basis of a subset of the data, which is then applied to further data, and revised, refined and reapplied. As we saw in Chapter 1, unlike some other thematic approaches to data analysis, Template Analysis does not stipulate in advance a set sequence of coding levels and researchers need not distinguish between themes on the basis of whether they are descriptive or interpretive if this is not helpful for them. In any case, King (2012) argues that the notion of a clear distinction between themes in terms of their being either 'descriptive' or 'interpretive' is debatable, though it is commonplace for early coding to mostly remain close to the data. The approach is very flexible with regards to the style and format of the template produced, leaving researchers able to develop their own coding structure in a design that best organizes and represents their themes in relation to their particular research aims: the central concern is that researchers are able to develop themes more extensively where the richest aspects of the data in relation to their research question are found (Brooks et al., 2015).

A final point worth making in relation to the structured but flexible approach to data encouraged by Template Analysis is that *all* qualitative analysis methods tend not in practice to move forward in the clearly delineated stages described in textbooks such as this one! Analysis often involves cycling back and forth between stages and this is especially true in Template Analysis because of its highly iterative nature. You should expect to repeat most of the procedural steps we describe below perhaps a number of times before you have finished the analysis of your data. Nevertheless, we would still argue that presenting a typical sequence of steps is useful in helping researchers to think about the direction of their analysis and the actions that will help them to take it forward. Our description below is therefore organized around the steps shown in Figure 3.1.

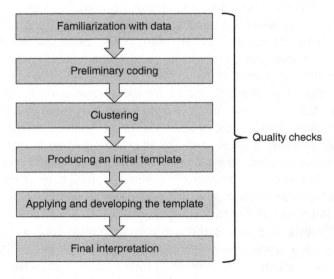

Figure 3.1 Typical steps in Template Analysis

FAMILIARIZING YOURSELF WITH YOUR DATA

As with most forms of qualitative analysis, the first step in Template Analysis is to familiarize yourself with your data set. If you are taking on the lengthy and arduous task of transcribing your own data (i.e. converting recorded material to text) rather than seeking outside transcription assistance, this can be a great opportunity to start the process of engagement with and reflection on your data set. How much (further) time you spend on familiarization will depend on the nature of your project. For instance, in a relatively small study (e.g. ten or fewer hour long interviews) it would be sensible to read through your full set of data at least once before proceeding. In a larger study, you might instead select a subset of accounts with which to start. The period of time available to you in which to complete your research will also play some part in determining when you need to move on from this stage. It is a good idea to ensure that if you are beginning with a subset of your data, that you choose items (transcripts, diary entries, field notes or whatever form your data are in) which represent a good cross-section of your whole data set. For example, if you are interviewing people from a number of different roles within an organization, it would make sense to ensure that the transcripts with which you choose to start analysis are not taken solely from one group. If your initial analysis is on a very homogenous sub-sample, you may find that early versions of your template are very hard to apply to subsequent data.

PRELIMINARY CODING

Again, this stage is essentially the same process as that used in most thematic approaches to coding qualitative data. You should begin to go through your data and start to identify anything in the text that seems likely to be helpful in contributing to your understanding of your research topic. Exactly how you do this is up to you, but a useful tip is to lay out your data in a way that facilitates the process and that helps you to easily locate particular segments of interest again. If you are using a computer software package (e.g. NVivo) to help with the analysis of your data, the program will have its own particular system to help carry out this stage. (We discuss the pros and cons of using computer software to help with Template Analysis later in this chapter.) If you are working by hand with, for example, interview transcripts, we would recommend double line spacing, with wide margins on each side of the page (perhaps 4-5 centimetres). Then you can read the text closely, highlighting anything of interest accompanied by a brief explanatory comment. You can use the margins of the page to write your comments next to the highlighted sections, or alternatively devise some kind of numbering system and compile your comments in a separate document. We strongly recommend using both page-numbering and line-numbering to help you

index your coding – you may well find that your word processor's line numbering function is by default set to start from '1' on each page; we find it helpful to change this to
'continuous' numbering throughout the document.

The next step is to use your preliminary comments to start defining potential
themes; it is worth considering at this point exactly what constitutes a theme in
Template Analysis. Given the popularity of thematic approaches to qualitative data,
King and Horrocks (2010) note that there is a surprising dearth of literature discussing and defining the term. Drawing on Braun and Clarke's (2006) exploration of
what constitutes a theme, King and Horrocks (2010) and King (2012) define a theme
as 'recurrent and distinctive features of participants' accounts, characterising particular perceptions and/or experiences, which the researcher sees as relevant to
the research question' (King and Horrocks, 2010: 150) and highlight the following
key features:

1. Themes are not objective facts, waiting to be uncovered in the data. Nor are they
    independent of the researcher who defines them – the process of identifying
    themes involves the researcher making choices about what to include, what to
    leave out and how to interpret the textual data. (Note that this is true even in the
    more realist forms of qualitative analysis.)
2. To be useful, themes should be relatively distinct from each other. Although some
    degree of overlap is inevitable, extensive overlapping between the themes you
    identify will be of little use in helping either you or your audience make any sense
    of your interpretation of the data.
3. Using the term 'theme' implies some level of repetition, and should not be applied
    to an isolated instance. Usually themes are identified across a number of cases or
    participant accounts, though you may find it useful to identify themes that recur
    within a single case, as this could indicate something of interest that distinguishes
    this one from all the other cases.

In some research projects, particularly when working in teams, we have found it useful to produce a document defining our themes, akin to a glossary of terms. Although
sometimes titles for themes suggest themselves readily, at other times it can take a
while to come up with a title which satisfactorily encompasses your meaning. This
period of reflection, during which you will need to carefully consider exactly what the
theme represents, can be useful in clarifying your thoughts and your interpretations.

Coding is the process undertaken by researchers through which they identify
themes in accounts and attach labels (codes) to index them (Brooks and King, 2014).
The terms 'theme' and 'code' are often used rather interchangeably, but it is worth
noting that in Template Analysis it is possible to have some codes which are neither
themes nor really serving to index themes. Codes can also be used to organize associated themes, serving as what Gibbs (2002) has termed 'placeholders'. King (2012)
uses a survey of staff views on the implementation of a new IT system to exemplify

this: in this instance, different staff groups might be used as placeholder codes under which themes relating to each group might be organized.

A *priori* themes

We briefly introduced the notion of *a priori* themes in Chapter 2, defining them as 'themes identified in advance of coding'. Preliminary coding is the stage at which a researcher may start utilizing any *a priori* codes they have defined at the outset of the research – although it is important to note here that while Template Analysis allows them, the use of *a priori* codes in Template Analysis is *not* obligatory. Whether or not you choose to use *a priori* codes, and how you might choose to use them, will depend on your particular piece of research. We will reflect on what might influence your choices in this respect now – and you can also refer back to Chapter 2 for more consideration of the ways in which the philosophical positioning of your work might also impact on the choices you make.

A *priori* themes are usually identified because a researcher has started out on a project with the intention of focusing on particular aspects of the phenomena under investigation. A *priori* themes may also be used when the importance of a particular issue in relation to a research question is already well established. Using *a priori* themes can be very useful indeed in accelerating the initial coding phase of analysis, a process which can often be rather time consuming.

A *priori* themes can be used in different ways, which may be thought of in terms of a continuum from 'hard' to 'soft'. By 'hard' *a priori* themes we mean those which are quite well developed and precisely defined. These may be useful if your study is focusing on particular evaluation criteria, or is informed by particular theoretical constructs. On the whole, studies taking a neo-positivist or limited realist approach are more likely to use 'hard' *a priori* themes than those from a contextualist or radical constructionist position (see Chapter 2). In contrast, 'soft' *a priori* themes are more loosely defined and often broader, representing potential aspects of the data in which you have an interest. They are rather like the notion of 'sensitizing concepts' that is used in constructivist Grounded Theory (Charmaz, 2014). In Chapter 4, we describe two specific research projects in which *a priori* themes were used in rather different ways. See also the three project examples given in the article we wrote with Serena McCluskey and Emma Turley (Brooks et al., 2015).

To lessen the possibility of *a priori* themes having any unwanted 'blinkering effect' on subsequent analysis (Brooks and King, 2014), they should generally be limited in number. In choosing any *a priori* themes, researchers should think carefully about their inclusion, ensuring that they clearly correspond to important concepts or perspectives in relation to the study and selecting them only after careful consideration of their research aims. Another key point to remember in relation to the use of *a priori* themes is that they should always be used tentatively. Researchers should be open to the possibility that, just as with other themes, *a priori* themes may not necessarily prove relevant, useful or meaningful as analysis proceeds and may need to be redefined or even discarded.

Using specialist software for coding

There exists now a wide range of specialist software products designed to assist in the process of qualitative analysis. Although they differ in some of the features they offer, all of them enable complex coding and searches. Some of the best-known and most widely used examples are NVivo, Atlas.ti and MAXQDA. The Online QDA site set up by Graham Gibbs provides summary details of many of the packages available and helpful discussion of many issues around the use of software in qualitative data analysis (http://onlineqda.hud.ac.uk). The structured and hierarchical nature of Template Analysis works well with most CAQDAS packages. In our own research we commonly use NVivo, though often we do the early stages of the analysis, up to production of the initial template, by hand. This is because we find that in familiarization and preliminary coding, working on a screen is more restrictive than having a hard copy of a transcript to flick back and forth through and to annotate with a fine pencil or highlighter pen. We also like to use Post-it notes on large sheets of paper attached to walls or flipcharts to develop theme clusters. However, as the template is applied to more data, and especially where multiple coders are involved, the software is very helpful. Crucially, it also means our final coding is saved electronically (with appropriate secure back-ups!) and can be searched very efficiently as we write up our research. Table 3.1 summarizes some of the main pros and cons of using CAQDAS in Template Analysis studies.

Table 3.1   Pros and cons of using CAQDAS for Template Analysis

Using CAQDAS: Pros	Using CAQDAS: Cons
Storage of analysis	Cost of software
Enables quick, complex searches	Time spent to learn software
Capacity to share analysis in team – e.g. some software has 'merge' facilities for multiple coders	Working on screen – especially in early stages, many researchers prefer to have hard copies they can flick back and forth through
Most software facilitates hierarchical coding	Tied to the computer
Visual modelling features in some software can work well with Template Analysis	Deeper levels of coding may be inefficient in some software (e.g. need to code text separately at each level of hierarchy)

If you do not have access to a CAQDAS package, or do not want to invest the time needed to learn to use one effectively, an alternative to purely hand-coding is to use other non-specialist software. Word processing programs such as Word or Apple's

Pages allow sections of text to be highlighted and comments boxes attached. This is potentially useful for preliminary coding. In fact, we sometimes use this facility to share early coding in a team – perhaps as part of a quality check – even when we are planning subsequently to use a CAQDAS software. Careful use of tables, header levels and numbering of paragraphs can be used to facilitate the later stages of analysis, though here CAQDAS has a clear advantage in terms of flexibility and power. Template versions can be written and developed in spreadsheets, with indexing to line-numbered transcripts (or other data items). Hahn (2008) describes in detail how to use word processing, database and spreadsheet software for qualitative analysis. His approach to coding is strongly influenced by Grounded Theory procedures, but much of his advice could also apply to Template Analysis. Dey (1993) also provides some useful advice, though of course the technical details of software are now very dated.

Writing case summaries

A potential limitation of all forms of thematic analysis is that they tend to fragment individual accounts of experience as they seek to examine patterns of themes across the data set as a whole. The larger the data set the more likely this is to happen. Your choice of a thematic approach such as Template Analysis should, of course, reflect a research question that is concerned with making sense of the experiences and/or views of your sample as a whole, rather than a highly idiographic focus on individual accounts. Nevertheless, retaining a sense of participants' perspectives in a more holistic way can be useful, both for making sure your themes 'work' in the context of their experiences as a whole and for providing examples to illustrate how the phenomenon you have studied is manifest in people's lives. (We discuss this latter point more in the section below on writing-up Template Analysis findings.)

One way in which this is commonly achieved in Template Analysis is for the researcher to write a brief case summary that captures the participant's story and (where relevant) the dynamics of the interview. Case summaries should where possible be written very soon after data collection. They should be impressionistic – giving a sense of the researcher's immediate response to the participant in contrast to the more rationalistic and systematic process of coding. In fact, we would particularly recommend that you make an effort to focus on those aspects of the interaction with the participant that are not readily addressed in coding. This could include such things as whether you found the person to be open or guarded, how well you felt they understood the aims of the research, or aspects of their physical presentation that were striking to you (if we are talking about a face-to-face method). Box 3.1 shows an example of a case summary.

Box 3.1 Example of a case summary

This interview was part of the 'Unpicking the threads' study, funded by Macmillan Cancer Research. The study examined how different types of nurses worked with each other, and with other professionals, patients and carers. It used the Pictor visual method (see King et al., 2013) to elicit examples of collaborative working in both cancer and long-term condition cases.

The example below was an interview conducted by team member David Wilde with a Community Matron (CM). This is a relatively new role, focused on co-ordinating care for patients with several long-term illnesses. This interview took place very early in the study. David focuses particularly on the interview process and researcher–participant relationship, to help learn lessons for future interviews as well as to inform subsequent analysis.

Interview with Community Matron (Kiara)

Kiara is the second CM I have interviewed. She had no information about the study prior to meeting me (unlike the first participant, who had been briefed slightly by a previous participant). So, there was an extended introduction and briefing about the study. She was a little reticent at first because she had the idea that we were wanting her to talk about palliative care patients she might be managing and as it happened not many of her clients were palliative/end-of-life, so she was a little worried she would be 'no good for what we were looking for'. After easing her worries about this, she seemed happy to take part with few questions. She too had previously done Pictor, although seemed to remember less about it than the first person interviewed. I got the impression that she was a bit nervous and very aware of the recorder to begin with. She hesitated over several things she felt she wanted to say and needed some coaxing along. But for most of the interview she talked quite freely and found the Pictor task enjoyable to do. She only did one Pictor task because she did not manage cancer patients. Her case mix consisted mostly of patients with a variety of respiratory problems and some heart failure patients. Kiara came to the CM role via a background working in the local acute hospital specializing with cardio-respiratory patients. She mentioned that the CM team was composed of members who had come through the District Nurse route and had gone into CM work because their job was threatened in some way, and others who came from non-nursing routes.

What was done well

I think I gave a much smoother and well-rounded introduction than in the previous interview. I felt that I had the 'shape' of the interview more firmly in mind and

I had drafted a one page bullet-pointed 'crib sheet' of procedural items prior to the interview and this worked much better than the more extensive notes I had been using in the first interview. These notes were handy also in helping me to remember when to pause and un-pause the recorder, which I was really worried about first time. I also referred less to the interview schedule than last time, especially later in the interview when certain questions about general collaborative working and how Kiara saw her role and the service developing in the future seemed to come much more naturally. Part of this I'm sure was the way Kiara was heading in terms of the topics she wanted to talk about, but I also had a better sense of where I wanted to probe in relation to her responses, which was quite different from the first interview I did, where I felt very conscious about asking all the questions. I managed to remember to mention the probes picked up from the first interview (role of support worker/healthcare assistants and upcoming restructuring of the service).

What was not done so well

I thought the interview went well overall. The fact that Kiara could not talk about a cancer case gave me a little concern, because, upon reflection and subsequent listening to the audio-recording, I felt that in the first interview I hadn't probed the respondent enough about her views concerning the potential similarities and differences between the two cases she had talked about. I was keen to put that right here and s**s law I wasn't able to! The fast turnaround between this interview and the next interview meant that I couldn't consolidate the chart straight away or write up any field notes. So, I felt that I was rushing into the next interview 'partially sighted', trying to remember the key points from this interview and what to probe in the next one.

CLUSTERING

Once you have identified themes in your textual data, you can begin to organize them into meaningful clusters, and start to think about how the themes relate to each other within and between clusters. This process should be very fluid as you explore different ways of organizing your themes. If you are using a priori themes, do not assume that these will necessarily be top-level themes heading up a particular cluster. You can move any and all of your themes around the emerging structure until you find a place for them where they seem to work best. In our work, we have often found it helpful at this stage to write our emerging themes on sticky (Post-it) notes, and to then place these on large (A0) sheets of paper so we can easily try out different ways of structuring and clustering the themes. If you use this method, we would advise that you line number all your transcripts (or other data items) and index on each sticky note the transcript and line number(s) where your evidence to support this potential theme can be found.

PRODUCING AN INITIAL TEMPLATE

Other methods of thematic qualitative data analysis can insist that preliminary coding is undertaken on the entire data set before you proceed further, but Template Analysis does not specify at what stage template formulation might begin. It is possible to wait until all data have undergone detailed preliminary coding before constructing an initial template, but it is normal for it to be developed on the basis of a subset of the data. We are often asked how may transcripts (or other data items) need to be included in the development of an initial template. There is no set answer to this; however, we can say that the more varied your data items are, the more you are likely to need to use. Thus, if you had 20 interviews with people who had generally very similar perspectives on the topic under study you might find that you felt confident to start developing the initial template after carrying out preliminary coding and clustering on four transcripts. In contrast, if the perspectives were very diverse, you might want to go through the earlier stages of analysis on eight of the transcripts before starting this stage. We have noted earlier that the boundaries between the main stages of Template Analysis are not really as clear cut as they appear in textbook accounts; that between *clustering* and *producing the initial template* are especially fuzzy. As you get more experienced with the technique you will often find you get a gut feeling for the right point at which to shift from one to the other.

The inherent danger in producing an initial template very early on in the analysis process is that you may become over-sensitized to material that easily 'fits' your template, neglecting material that cannot be as readily encompassed. Even after you have defined an initial coding template, you should continue to keep an open mind when approaching new data to develop the template further and be ready to modify the template as necessary. Nonetheless, there are recognized advantages in starting template development somewhat early, not least of which may be pragmatic (for example, in a project with a particularly tight deadline or a large number of participants it may be impractical to wait until all data has undergone preliminary analysis before proceeding with template formulation). Proceeding earlier with the formulation of an initial template can allow you to focus in on those areas of greatest relevance to your research, avoiding potentially lengthy repetitious and/or redundant coding.

A key feature of Template Analysis is its emphasis on hierarchical coding, whereby groups of similar codes are clustered together to produce more general higher order themes. Hierarchical coding allows for analysis of the textual data at varying levels of specificity, and for researchers to focus in greater detail on areas of particular interest or meaning in relation to their research aims. Top-level or main themes may be elaborated in some detail through the use of sub-themes, and there can be as many levels of coding as the researcher deems helpful in exploring their research question (it is worth noting that depth rather than breadth of coding can often prove useful in the identification of fine distinctions in key areas). Rather than stipulating a set number of coding levels, or a predetermined sequence in which coding should proceed, researchers using Template Analysis are instead encouraged to explore in most depth those areas which seem particularly rich in terms of the insight they provide into the topic area of interest. One would expect to see these top-level themes developed further in terms of the number and levels of sub-themes, although it is important also to keep in mind the final project goal – clarifying the mass of qualitative data obtained. Researchers should endeavour to keep in mind the true aims of their work even at these early stages of analysis, and to remember that template construction and templates themselves are a means to an end, rather than the final goal of the work.

There needs to be some balance between depth of coding in the analysis process, and the organization and interpretation of data in the final stages of the project. Template Analysis allows *parallel coding* – coding the same segment of text with two or more distinct themes. Our only note of caution here would be that if certain themes very often end up being used in parallel, you should ask yourself whether they actually relate to different aspects of the research topic, or whether they might usefully be merged into a single theme.

While the emphasis in Template Analysis is on hierarchical organization of themes, coding templates may also highlight lateral relationships across thematic clusters. Themes which permeate several thematic clusters are known as *integrative themes*. Integrative themes can be thought of as undercurrents running through participants' accounts – integrative themes may not even be explicitly raised or addressed by participants, but nonetheless can be seen on careful reading of the data to pervade participants' discussion of the research topic. For example, in our evaluation of an end-of-life care service (Brooks and King, 2014), we found that the unique approach and special characteristics of this particular service was a theme which clearly permeated and connected our other identified top-level themes. In our final template, we therefore used 'What makes this service special?' as an integrative theme indicating the typical attitude to the service evident in all our participants' accounts.

APPLYING AND DEVELOPING THE TEMPLATE

Once you have formulated an initial template, the next stage in the analysis process is to go back to your data and apply it to fresh material. This involves working systematically through your data set, identifying segments of text that are relevant to your research question and marking them with the relevant code (or perhaps codes) so that they are clearly denoted as relating to one or more of the thematic categories making up your template. Where there is material of potential relevance to your research question in the data, you need to now consider whether any of the themes defined on your initial template can be used to represent this material. Where the existing themes on your template do not readily incorporate the new data, it may be necessary to modify your template. Modifications can include inserting new themes, redefining existing themes, merging themes, changing the scope of themes (e.g. moving from a top level to a lower level in the coding structure) and perhaps even deleting themes if they seem redundant. You could if you wish reorganize your template after examining each new account, but in practice it is more common to work through several accounts, noting possible revisions as you go, before constructing a new version of the template. So you might for example undertake preliminary analysis on five interview transcripts before formulating an initial template. You might then apply this template to a further three transcripts before producing a revised template for application to further data.

There is no fixed number of iterations involved in this application of successive versions of your template to your data, and the length of time you continue with this stage will depend on your particular project and the data you have obtained. You should continue trying out successive versions of the template, modifying as necessary, and trying out again until you are happy that you have a 'final version' template which provides a rich and comprehensive representation of your data. Obviously, time and resource limitations are likely to have some bearing on the number of iterations possible, but it is important that your analysis and final template do not leave any data clearly relevant to your research question uncoded. Arguably, 'final version' template is somewhat of a misnomer, as continued engagement with the data always has the potential to identify further potential refinements to coding. However, on a pragmatic level, you will at some point need to decide whether you have produced a version of your template which satisfactorily meets the needs of your particular project, taking into account the time and other resources available to you. It is always possible to revisit the template at a later date for another purpose – for example, we have sometimes found that a template which works well to assist in data interpretation for a specific purpose (e.g. an evaluation report of a service) can then be revisited and refined in some detail to produce another template version to help with the analysis of the data for an academic journal article.

It is worth noting that the systematic nature of Template Analysis can be very useful in providing an audit trail to demonstrate the quality of your data analysis. The methodical process of applying and modifying your template can be documented so as to record your emerging thinking through the analysis process. We recommend keeping a full record of how the template develops, numbering and dating each version of your template. We would also recommend making some accompanying notes to document any major changes you have made to successive versions of your template, and explaining your reasoning for these changes.

When you have a 'final version' template, it is time to revisit your original data set once more and apply your final template to the whole data set. Once this is complete, your template can now provide the basis for your interpretation of your data, as well as being a useful guide when it comes to structuring and writing up your research findings.

FINAL INTERPRETATION

As we noted earlier in this chapter, producing a template and using it to code your data does not represent the end of your work when using Template Analysis in a piece of qualitative research. Once you have finished this process, your task is now to develop your final interpretation of your coded data and present an account of this. Exactly how you go about doing this will depend on the aims, philosophical position and content of your particular piece of work. There are, however, a few useful generic guidelines we can offer.

Examining patterns of themes in your data

Simply summarizing your main findings under each thematic heading and presenting this as your final write up is likely to result in a dreary and not especially insightful final piece. However, listing themes can be a useful process to go through as a first stage. Doing this can enable you to examine how codes are distributed within and between your pieces of textual data, which can in turn alert you to aspects of the data warranting further examination. For example, if certain themes feature prominently in all your interview transcripts from a subset of your sample, but rarely or never in the accounts obtained from another subset of your sample, it might be revealing to examine this more closely – might it, for instance, indicate some important difference in views between the two groups? It is important to note here that frequency and pattern of theme distribution do not on their own reveal anything meaningful – they merely highlight areas potentially worthy of closer examination for you to consider.

Prioritizing themes

Even in a relatively modest scale qualitative study using Template Analysis, you are likely to generate more themes than you can talk about in any detail in a Master's dissertation – let alone in journal articles, reports to organizations and so on. In any case, some themes, and some clusters of themes, are likely to provide much more insight into the topic you are investigating than others. Prioritizing the themes you need to examine in the greatest depth is therefore essential. To help you think about which themes you need to concentrate on, we would suggest you consider the following:

- the relevance of themes, and/or links between themes, to your research question
- themes that contradict common assumptions and/or conclusions in the existing literature; including those which surprise you by their lack of prominence
- themes that distinguish between groups of participants in meaningful ways.

While you do need to be selective in prioritizing the themes on which you choose to focus, this has to be balanced against an equally pressing need to remain open to your data. We have emphasized the importance of remembering and focusing on your research question and your research aims throughout the analysis process, but it would be a mistake to immediately disregard themes that are not of obvious and direct relevance to your initial research question without at least some consideration and thought. Even themes that are of seemingly marginal relevance can play an important role in contextualizing the study and need not necessarily require lengthy explication. It may be somewhat more difficult to decide whether to include or omit a theme which is evidently important to participants, but which does not seem to relate to the identified aims of your study. In this instance, you should consider whether or not such a theme assists in understanding of any of the central themes – if it does, then we recommend that you include it in your interpretation.

Finding and developing connections

Beyond looking for patterns and the relative importance of themes in addressing your research question(s), it is often especially useful to explore how themes relate to each other (in addition to the hierarchical relationships within clusters). At the simplest, this may involve noting that certain themes tend to coincide in the data and considering what this says about the subject under investigation. If you have identified integrative or other lateral themes, these should also give you insights into connections within the data. You may wish to take this process further to develop a model of the phenomenon you are investigating or to critique and propose revisions to an existing theoretical model (e.g. Shaw and Wainwright, 2007; McCluskey et al., 2011).

Finally, you may choose to deepen your analysis by incorporating other forms alongside Template Analysis. Drawing on case summaries alongside the thematic coding can be useful, as noted above. You can take this further by carrying out a narrative analysis of some or all of your cases, or you could incorporate other methods where they fit with your overall aims and position, such as a discourse-based method. There is a growing interest in mixing qualitative approaches – a strategy sometimes referred to as 'qualitative pluralism'; see Frost et al. (2010) and Pritchard (2012) for more discussion of this.

QUALITY CHECKS

Quality criteria in qualitative analysis

In order to persuade those reading your work of the value of your research, you may well want to carry out one or more forms of quality check on your analysis. Before you can consider the quality procedures you should use, you need to decide on quality criteria suited to your research. As Johnson et al. (2006) argue, in qualitative research we need to select criteria that are coherent to the different philosophical positions taken by different approaches – criteria that are appropriate for a neo-positivist study may well not make sense for a contextualist study, for example. We have already touched on this issue in our discussion of the main philosophical positions in Chapter 2. Broadly speaking, those discussing quality criteria for qualitative research tend to suggest three approaches. Firstly, we can apply, perhaps with some adaptation, the criteria used in quantitative research – especially validity and reliability. Secondly, we can use alternative criteria designed specifically for qualitative research. Thirdly, we may argue that general criteria are inappropriate and that the quality of analysis must be judged within the setting of a particular study.

With regard to the use of criteria from quantitative research, discussion mostly focuses on *reliability* and *validity*. Many writers suggest that reliability is not an appropriate criterion in qualitative research, because it is intrinsically concerned with issues of measurement. For instance, Blumberg et al. (2014: 495) define reliability as 'a characteristic of measurement concerned with accuracy, precision and consistency'. With regard to qualitative research, we would argue that it is really only a suitable criterion for studies taking a qualitative neo-positivist position (as described in Chapter 2) where the researcher is using a realist epistemology. In such a case a researcher might legitimately want to show the 'accuracy' of coding categories by using statistical inter-rater reliability scores, as in the study by Kidd (2008) which we discuss in Chapter 5.

Validity is a more complex concept than reliability. In quantitative research it is common to specify several different types of validity with which a researcher needs to be concerned; for example, Bryman and Bell (2015) refer to *measurement validity*, *internal validity*, *external validity* and *ecological validity*. In qualitative research, validity is most commonly used in a way that corresponds to the notion of ecological validity – the extent to which the research context is congruent with the real-world context of the phenomenon under investigation (Braun and Clarke, 2013). Validity is clearly a suitable quality criterion for qualitative neo-positivist research. It is also applicable to limited realist studies, given their adherence to a realist ontology, though writers in this tradition may recast the concept to take account of their constructivist epistemology. Maxwell (2012), for example, refers to *descriptive*, *interpretive* and *theoretical* validity. Contextualist and radical constructionist positions have more problems with the notion of validity, as they do not believe in a single, knowable external reality. Commonly researchers taking such positions argue for alternative quality criteria (e.g. Denzin and Lincoln, 2005), or dismiss the idea of fixed criteria altogether.

There have been numerous attempts to define alternative criteria, in line with the second approach above. These include general criteria, which aim to be relevant to any qualitative research (e.g. Lincoln and Guba, 1985; Lincoln, 1995; Spencer et al., 2003; Yardley, 2008; Tracy, 2010), and criteria designed for specific disciplines, methods or philosophical positions (e.g. Johnson et al., 2006; Creswell, 2007). An interesting approach taken by Cassell et al. (2005) was to derive criteria empirically, by interviewing stakeholders within qualitative management research about what they identified as implicit and explicit criteria for good qualitative research in business and management research. They carried out a Template Analysis on these interviews and categorized detailed descriptors of quality under three top-level themes: quality output, quality process and quality performance.

The debates around quality criteria continue in business and management research, and qualitative research more widely. We will not support one set of criteria or one specific approach to defining criteria here; rather, we would agree with Symon and Cassell (2012: 221) that you should identify criteria relevant to your approach and justify them explicitly:

> qualitative researchers should draw on those elements of quality that they think are most relevant to their own research and be careful in their writings to indicate to potential assessors what the aims of the research were and therefore how it should be judged.

Procedures for qualitative analysis quality checks

Once you have identified appropriate criteria for your research approach, you need to consider how you will go about demonstrating quality against them. There is a wide range of strategies that can be used to ensure the quality of analysis in qualitative research. Often the same strategy may be used in different ways to address different types of quality criteria, as we will discuss below – especially with regard to independent coding and respondent feedback. We will highlight how each strategy may be employed in the context of Template Analysis. Note that our focus here is very much on quality assessment that directly relates to the analysis process. This is only part of the task of demonstrating quality – you also need to think about how your research design choices and the way you write up your study contribute to a high quality project. Table 3.2 summarizes some of the main strategies you may choose to use to assess quality in Template Analysis.

Table 3.2 Quality check procedures in Template Analysis

Procedure	When to use	How to use
Independent coding	At preliminary coding stage, and/or after development of the initial template	You may use fellow students, your supervisor or a panel of people with expertise in your area to do this. Provide independent coder(s) with a sample of data – e.g. one transcript, or long extracts from two or three transcripts (if using interviews). Also provide them with written instructions for the coding task – if they are not familiar with qualitative analysis, you might need to outline the key principles to them first. Meet to compare and contrast your coding. If doing the check at preliminary coding stage, the focus should be on considering whether the themes emerging in your analysis seem plausible and whether your coder(s) have identified aspects you have missed. You may also want to check whether they have found any *a priori* themes to be useful. If at the template development stage, the focus should be on clarity of the template, how well it encompasses the data, and where changes may need to be made.
Respondent feedback	Most likely to be useful at later stages of template development	There is considerable debate about the place of respondent feedback in quality procedures. Some see it as very valuable while others warn that we should not expect participants to in effect stand outside themselves and judge the analysis. There may also be ethical issues to consider. However, even if your approach would not allow respondent feedback to be seen as any kind of 'validation', it may still be useful as an additional level of data that may give you fresh insights into your interpretation. To employ respondent feedback you could provide participants with coded extracts of their data – at one or more stages of the Template Analysis process – and ask them to comment on what rings true, what doesn't make sense, what they disagree with, and so on. This could be done in writing or face-to-face with their comments audio-recorded. As with independent coders, you are likely to need to provide some basic training/instruction in the task you are asking them to carry out.
Keeping an audit trail	Throughout the analysis process	An 'audit trail' is a record of the way your analysis developed, and the key analytical decisions you made. Template Analysis lends itself very well to keeping an audit trail, as you can (and should!) retain dated versions of the template to which you can easily add comments explaining why particular modifications were made. These may include reflexive comments on how your own position shaped coding choices and/or template development.
Thick description and use of participant quotes	At draft write-up stage	The notion of 'thick description' was introduced into ethnographic research by Geertz (1973) and promoted more widely in qualitative research by Lincoln and Guba (1985). It refers to the notion that qualitative researchers should provide sufficient detail about the context of the phenomena they are studying to enable a reader to judge how conclusions drawn may apply more widely. For a qualitative project using Template Analysis, you need to ensure that you have described your research setting and your main themes clearly and thoroughly. We would suggest you ask a 'critical friend' and/or your supervisor to consider this at the early draft stages of your write-up.

WRITING UP

Styles of presentation for Template Analysis findings

At the end of all your analytic work, you need to write up your analysis and present a coherent account of the interpretation you have made of your data. There are a number of ways you can approach your write up, and the way you go about doing this will inevitably be constrained by the nature of your data, the type of document you want to produce (theses and dissertations will face differing format constraints from an academic journal article, for example) and your intended readership. Below we describe three broad approaches to presenting a Template Analysis study. Whichever approach you choose, remember that the use of direct or verbatim quotes from participants is essential. It is usually a good idea to include both short quotes which help your reader understand specific interpretations you are making as well as longer quotes which can allow readers to get some sense of the original or raw data.

The first approach you can use to present your work is as a series of individual case studies followed by a discussion of similarities and differences between cases. If you wrote case summaries for your participants early in the research process, these can be helpful to draw on alongside the thematic coding within each participant's data. The advantage of this is that readers are able to clearly discern individuals' perspectives. This approach requires there to be sufficient space available to provide adequate descriptions of individual cases and is less useful with larger numbers of participants when it runs the risk of becoming repetitive and confusing for the reader. The second approach is to structure your account around the main themes identified, using verbatim quotes or examples taken from your data set to exemplify your line of reasoning. The great majority of published articles using Template Analysis follow this style; it is an efficient way to present your findings, and foregrounds the main themes upon which your discussion will focus. However, this approach – focusing on across-case rather than within-case analysis – can potentially lead to over-generalization and some loss of holistic understanding in relation to the accounts of individual partici-pants. You can sometimes overcome this limitation by adopting the third approach, in effect a synthesis of the two approaches already described. This third alternative approach combines a thematic presentation of findings with a small number of case studies to illustrate the key themes. The challenge when using this approach is to choose cases in a way that fairly represents themes in the overall data set.

Presenting your template

If your 'final' template is quite extensive, you may find that it is not practical to include the whole thing in the main body of your thesis or of journal articles arising from it. Sometimes, it is possible to include a simplified version (perhaps the top two levels of themes, for example) and include a more detailed template as an appendix. We would emphasize, though, that your template can have an important and useful communicative function, and it is therefore worth taking some time to consider how best you might display it in your work.

While templates can be presented in whatever way a researcher finds best to help communicate their analysis, there are two main styles that tend to be used: (1) as a linear 'list' presentation and (2) as a diagrammatic 'mind map'. In the first of these, themes are straightforwardly presented in a list. Various techniques can be used in the layout of the template on the page (e.g. indentation; typography – that is, size and/or style of font; a numbering system) to make the different levels of coding evident to readers. This style tends to take up less space than a diagrammatic representation of the template and most published work using Template Analysis tends to use this linear format. However, a diagrammatic representation can be especially useful if you want to clearly display lateral links between thematic clusters. In this sort of 'mind map' style format, you can use connecting arrows as well as typographic effects to indicate coding levels. There is also the option of using this style for your own purposes, but then converting your template into a list format in your write up if need be. Figures 3.2 and 3.3 show the template from one study displayed in the two different styles. These are from a project looking at the process of supervision in a multi-disciplinary primary care team (King et al., 2000), including a family doctor (GP) and three nurses in different roles. Note that the 'mind map' format in Figure 3.3 only displays some of the main themes, underlining the point that this style requires more space to display.

---

1. Issues re. Model of supervision

    1.1 Contract
    1.2 Comparison with other approaches
    1.3 Use of 'reflexive cycle' diagram
    1.4 Training
    1.5 Familiarity with ...

2. Practicalities

    2.1 Timing issues
    2.2 Length of sessions
    2.3 Location of sessions

3. Group dynamics

    3.1 Atmosphere/climate
         3.1.1 Formal/informal
         3.1.2 Tense/relaxed
         3.1.3 Focused/unfocused

(Continued)

Figure 3.2   (Continued)

> 3.2 Cohesiveness
>   3.2.1 Group as a whole
>   3.2.2 Sub-groups
>   3.2.2.1 Nurse/doctor
>   3.2.2.2 Practice-based/pratice-attached
> 3.3 Issues of power and authority
>
> 4. Roles in the group supervision process
>
>   4.1 Supervisee's role
>   4.1 1 Issues brought (what and why)
>   4.1.2 Comfort with role
>   4.1.3 Helpfulness (or not) of group members' contributions
>   4.2. Facilitator's role
>   4.2.1 Comfort with role
>   4.2.2 Style adopted (inc. adherence to model)
>   4.2.3 Clarity of role
>   4.3. Group member/supervisor's role
>   4.3.1 Comfort with role
>   4.3.2 Nature of interventions
>   4.3.2.1 Type
>   4.3.2.2 Frequency
>   4.3.3 Clarity of role
>
> 5. Outcomes
>
>   5.1 Progress re. issues brought
>   5.1.1 Own
>   5.1.2 Others'
>   5.2 Discussion about outcomes
>   5.3 Mutual understanding (or lack of)
>   5.3.1 Yours of others
>   5.3.2 Others' of you
>   5.4 Support
>
> 6. Future involvement in MDCS
>
>   6.1 Desire (or not) for future involvement
>   6.2 Possible changes
>   6.2.1 ... in membership
>   6.2.2 ... in format
>   6.2.3 ... in preparation/training
>
> 7. Non-participants' views of MDCS
>
>   7.1 Uncertainty
>   7.2 Lack of awareness
>   7.3 Questions re. its progress
>
> 8. Practice characteristics
>
>   8.1 Others' expectations
>   8.2 Staff characteristics
>   8.3 Values

Figure 3.2   Example of template displayed in linear style

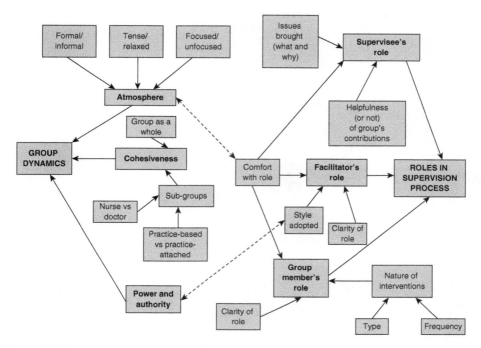

Figure 3.3 Example of template displayed in 'mind map' style

CHAPTER SUMMARY

In this chapter we have taken you through the procedural steps involved in using Template Analysis. We have outlined the six main steps in the method:

1. familiarization with the data
2. preliminary coding
3. clustering
4. producing an initial template
5. applying and developing the template
6. final interpretation.

In the course of this we have considered:

- the use of *a priori* themes
- the use of specialist software in coding.

We have concluded with a consideration of quality checks and of how to write up findings from a Template Analysis study.

4

CASE EXAMPLES OF THE USE OF TEMPLATE ANALYSIS

INTRODUCTION

So far we have explained the place of Template Analysis in business and management research, highlighted the philosophical issues associated with the choice of this method, and taken you through a nuts-and-bolts description of how to carry it out. We hope you now feel well prepared to begin using Template Analysis on your own data. As experienced teachers of qualitative methods, however, we would strongly emphasize how valuable it can be to look closely at how others have used a method before you venture to use it yourself. We have written the next two chapters of this book with this point very much in mind. In Chapter 5 we look at a wider range of ways in which the Template Analysis technique has been used across the business and management research literature.

In the present chapter we show you two detailed case examples based on how we have employed Template Analysis in our own research. So that you can better apply these examples to your own work, we have adapted them to present them as the work of two fictional Master's students (David and Nasifah). The original research projects on which these examples are based are available for those interested in finding out more (see McCluskey et al., 2011; Brooks et al., 2013; Brooks et al., 2015).

Case study 4.1   Work participation and back pain

Background to the study

Back pain is a leading cause of disability in the United Kingdom, especially in adults of working age (Palmer et al., 2000). The National Health Service spends more than £1 billion per year on back pain related costs (Maniadakis and Gray, 2000) but the indirect costs of reduced work capacity due to chronic back pain far outweigh direct medical costs (Phillips et al., 2008). Clinical guidelines for the management of back pain emphasize the importance of remaining active (Van Tulder and Koes, 2002) and vocational rehabilitation research suggests that remaining in work, or returning to work as soon as possible, is better for patients, limiting the potential negative social, psychological and physical effects of long-term sickness absence (Waddell and Burton, 2006; Waddell et al., 2008). Fewer than half those individuals disabled for longer than six months return to work, and after two years' absence from work, the return-to-work rate is close to zero (Spitzer et al., 1987). It is thought that social influences may play an important role in determining whether or not individuals with a back condition are able to maintain or resume work participation (e.g. McCluskey et al., 2011; Brooks et al., 2013).

The researcher and their project

For our purposes here, we shall assume that this study was undertaken by David. David is a Business and Management student who is required to undertake an independent research project as part of his Master's studies. David has a particular interest in personnel and HR issues. He has decided to look at some of the issues which might affect an individual's capacity to return to work after suffering either a back injury or some kind of back pain, and is interested in exploring the role family members might play in this respect. In his study, David interviewed people who had been off work for a prolonged period of time due to chronic back pain. He also asked his back pain sufferer participants to nominate a close adult family member – their *significant other* (SO) – to participate with them in the study. The aim of David's study was to explore how both back pain sufferers and their significant others thought about and responded to the patient's back pain, with a particular focus on employment and work issues.

The analysis process

Philosophical position

Using the categorization of philosophical positions that we presented in Chapter 2, this project can be seen as taking a qualitative neo-positivist position. This was appropriate for David as he wanted to draw heavily on existing theory, as described below, directly informing his analysis with constructs from the theory.

Getting to know the data

As we described in Chapter 3, the first step in undertaking Template Analysis is to familiarize yourself with your data set. In this study, David undertook separate interviews with five back pain patients and five significant others, giving him a data set consisting of ten interviews all lasting around one hour. He was able to complete data collection in full before he proceeded with analysis and could therefore read through the entire ten-hour data set before he began any coding. This provided him with a good opportunity to start engaging with his data, and to start thinking about themes emerging that might be included in an initial template.

Mode of analysis

At the start of his analysis, David discussed with his supervisor whether to use a CAQDAS package. He realized there would be a cost in terms of time to learn the software, but also an advantage in the power of the program to enable complex searches and comparisons. In the end, the deciding factor for him was that he was considering undertaking a PhD at some point in the future, so felt that learning how to use CAQDAS would be valuable. At his supervisor's suggestion, he carried out the stages up to construction of the initial template by hand, and the first iteration by hand. He then entered data into the CAQDAS package for further development of the template and final interpretation of the data.

Preliminary coding and use of a *priori* themes

Research exploring illness beliefs is often quantitative, using questionnaire measures to ask participants what they think about their symptoms and the impact of their condition on everyday life. In this study, David wanted a more in-depth understanding of the issues involved and used qualitative research methods – interviews – to explore beliefs about and experiences of back pain in relation to employment with both patients and a family member. However, to ensure that his research linked with and was able to build on mainstream theory, David used an existing widely used and very well validated questionnaire measure of illness beliefs – the Illness Perception Questionnaire or IPQ (Moss-Morris et al., 2002) – to design his interview schedule. When it came to undertaking preliminary coding on his data, David kept in mind that he was particularly interested in exploring parts of the transcript which related to questions posed in the original questionnaire measure.

In this study, David was therefore able to identify nine *a priori* themes in advance of coding, all taken from the subscales of the questionnaire measure he had used as a basis for designing his interview. In Chapter 3, we described how a document defining themes can be useful in analysis to refer back to when coding. This was a technique utilized in this particular study, and David produced a short document providing a clear definition for each of the nine *a priori* themes (as he was dealing with constructs taken from a widely used model, producing clear and succinct definitions was not problematic). Figure 4.1 shows David's nine initial *a priori* themes, together with the theme definitions he used at this stage of the work.

---

(1)   Illness identity (*the label of the illness and the symptoms viewed as being part of the condition*)

(2)   Beliefs about causality (*personal ideas about cause, which may include simple single causes or more complex multiple causal models*)

(3)   Beliefs about timeline (acute/chronic) (*how long it is believed the illness will last – time-limited or long-term*)

(4)   Beliefs about timeline (cyclical) (*beliefs regarding nature of condition – are symptoms episodic or constant?*)

(5)   Beliefs about consequences of back pain (*expected/experienced effects and outcomes*)

(6)   Beliefs about personal control of back pain (*to what extent can the patient control/ manage the condition?*)

(7)   Beliefs about treatment control of back pain (*to what extent can treatments control/ manage the condition?*)

(8)   Emotional representations (not a *proxy indicator of general mood – rather, emotional responses generated by the illness condition*)

(9)   Illness coherence (*the extent to which individual has a coherent understanding of condition – can be thought of as a type of meta-cognition reflecting way in which respondent evaluates coherence of illness belief*)

Figure 4.1   David's *a priori* themes and definitions

Preliminary coding proceeded as described in Chapter 3. David chose a transcript of an interview undertaken with a significant other participant to begin, and read through the transcript looking for anything in the text that seemed relevant to his research topic. He did this simply by reading through a hard copy transcript, highlighting or underlining any sections that seemed interesting or relevant and using the margin to make some brief explanatory notes (see Figure 4.2). As he was working with an existing theoretical framework to structure his analysis, David ensured that he kept his nine *a priori* themes in mind even at this early stage.

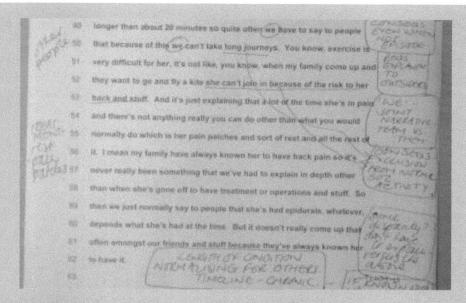

Figure 4.2 Example of David's preliminary coding

Formulating David's initial template

As Template Analysis does not specify at what stage template formulation should begin, it is up to the individual researcher to decide when it is appropriate to produce an initial template. Given that David had a rather extensive list of relatively well-defined *a priori* themes in advance of coding in this study, he felt able to proceed with the design of an initial template using a subset of his entire data set. He began template formulation having undertaken preliminary coding on two transcripts, both taken from interviews with significant others. As we noted in Chapter 3, it is important to think carefully about the data you choose to use in these early stages so as not to 'skew' your template design, which can be problematic later in the coding process. David's familiarity with the data set was advantageous at this point – he was confident that the transcripts he had chosen were not atypical of the remainder of his data set. David considered the options available to him in terms of how to approach analysis, and a variety of ways in which he could consider his sample and select transcripts. He could think about 'dyads' and code their data together. Alternatively, he could code patient participants to one template and significant other participants separately. In deciding how to approach this, David thought carefully about *why* he had undertaken this work. There is much more known about the illness beliefs of patients themselves than there is about the illness beliefs of significant others in this context – and there is especially little work that focuses on the significant other's *own* perspective in this respect.

Given that this was a novel aspect of his research, and one he was particularly interested in exploring, David decided to focus on the significant other participants first. In fact, he was able to use the same template for all participants but he did take care in analysis to ensure that he was not shoe-horning data into a template that worked well for one group and not another. That David was able to do this is in line with previous research suggesting that dyads often hold similar beliefs and have similar narratives with regards to illness (e.g. Figueiras and Weinman, 2003; Brooks et al., 2014).

Although his analysis began with nine *a priori* themes, it quickly became apparent to David that he could merge some of his thematic categories for the purposes of constructing a template. For example, he decided to replace the two top-level themes 'Beliefs about timeline (acute/chronic)' (*a priori* theme (3) in Figure 4.1) and 'Beliefs about timeline (cyclical)' (*a priori* theme (4) in Figure 4.1) with a single top-level theme. As his patient participants were all considered to have a chronic condition, it worked better to have one top-level timeline theme and to use sub-themes under this category to cover finer and more detailed coding relating to chronicity and the episodic nature of pain. He also expanded his definition of this thematic category to include reflections on the ageing process.

David's coding had already begun to identify other themes in addition to his *a priori* themes which were of interest. For example, he included an additional theme entitled 'Interacting with the world' on his initial template – this theme encompassed participants' reflections on dealings with healthcare professionals and with other people in relation to the patient's pain condition, as well as talk about the intertwining of patient and significant other health problems (interestingly, it emerged that all the significant others interviewed had chronic health problems themselves). Although this theme does not appear on his final version of the template, it was a useful category at this stage for identifying these issues (in later versions of the template, these were reclassified as sub-themes under different thematic headings).

David carried out a quality check by asking a student colleague to independently code long extracts from two transcripts (one sufferer and one significant other), using the initial template. The colleague, Sarah, had some familiarity with qualitative research already, so did not need extensive explanation of the task. However, David did give her a 'codebook' with definitions of the top-level themes on the initial template, plus those lower-level themes which he thought may not be self-explanatory. David and Sarah met to discuss who their coding compared; on the basis of this, David concluded that the initial template would allow a valid interpretation of the data, though he did make some minor changes to lower-level themes where lack of clarity and potential overlap were identified by Sarah.

Developing and applying David's template

Once David had developed an initial template, he began applying this to his data set. He used a large room with plenty of space and big tables. On the tables he had AO flipchart paper, a separate sheet for each of his *a priori* themes plus additional sheets for any other emerging themes (Figure 4.3 shows some of these). His themes were written on Post-it notes, allowing him to shift them around however he so chose. Even though David had already refined his *a priori* themes to some extent, they were still considered as tentative. He was prepared and willing to discard, redefine or reposition any of his initial themes should the need arise.

Figure 4.3 Early coding to David's initial template

David went through each transcript identifying segments of text that related to his research aims, and coded segments either to his *a priori* themes or, where appropriate, started thinking about additional new thematic categories. He wrote quotes (and line numbers) on his sticky notes, and then added these to his AO sheets. After each coding session, David typed up the template so that he had an ongoing record which enabled him to see how his analysis was developing.

At the point where David had produced a second full iteration of the template, as noted above he moved his analysis into a CAQDAS program. This involved him in setting up the template in the software, entering all the transcripts and coding to each theme. CAQDAS enabled rapid and complex searching of the data to assist further development of the template – for example, looking at where certain themes overlapped to consider whether they were usefully distinct from each other. As analysis proceeded, David continued to refine his top-level themes.

For example, he merged the two 'control' thematic headings (themes (6) and (7) in Figure 4.1) with one overarching 'Beliefs about curability, control and management' theme. It was clear to David that for this particular chronic pain condition which had become part of our participants' everyday lives, interviewees did not distinguish between treatment control and personal control in their talk – for example, decisions about whether or not to take painkillers to alleviate pain were often described as a self-management strategy and a personal choice of the back pain sufferer and he couldn't simply distinguish between this as a treatment or personal means of symptom control

David also decided to reclassify one of his initial *a priori* themes – the 'illness coherence' theme – as an integrative theme. As we discussed in Chapter 3, it may sometimes be appropriate in Template Analysis to highlight lateral relationships across thematic clusters as well as thinking about the hierarchical organization of themes in a template. Integrative themes are themes which permeate several thematic clusters. It was evident to David as he proceeded with analysis that 'illness coherence' (the extent to which participants felt themselves to have a clear understanding of the illness condition) permeated almost every other thematic category. For example, his 'Beliefs about curability, control and management' theme included sub-themes around uncertainties with regards to symptom management and treatment which he also coded as relating to 'illness coherence'; 'Expectations about timeline' included sub-themes around the unpredictability of pain episode onset which he similarly saw as a facet of 'Illness coherence'. Rather than identifying it as a main theme, it seemed more meaningful for his purposes to consider 'Illness coherence' as an integrative theme cutting across all other themes which pervaded participants' discussion of living with and managing a chronic condition.

The final template

David's final coding template (see Figure 4.4) was comprised of eight top-level hierarchical themes. Six of these were *a priori* themes (illness identity; beliefs about causality; expectations about timeline; perceived consequences of back pain; control, management and treatment of back pain; emotional representations). In addition to these, he also had two extra top-level themes which emerged through his analysis. The first of these was 'Impact on/influence of significant other'. It related both to how significant others influenced the sufferers' experiences of pain and incapacity, and how the latter's experiences impacted on significant other. It sought to capture the intertwined nature of the two parties' experiences. His second additional top-level theme – 'Claimant as genuine' – referred to the evident need of participants' to demonstrate the genuine nature of the patient's back pain condition.

1. Illness identity

1.1 Physical symptoms
    1.1.1 Pain
    1.1.2 Other symptoms (directly attributed to back condition)
    1.1.3 Other symptoms (not directly attributed to back condition/indirect or unclear attribution)/co-morbidity
1.2 Intrinsic vagueness of condition/incomprehension
1.3 Labelled by condition

2. Causality (beliefs about initial cause and subsequent onsets)

2.1 Initial onset
    2.1.1 Previous work/certain types of work
    2.1.2 Innocuous activity
    2.1.3 Hereditary condition
    2.1.4 Specific physiological causality
    2.1.5 Chance causes
    2.1.6 Unknown cause
2.2 Subsequent onset 'triggers'
    2.2.1 Unpredictable onsets/wide variation of 'triggers'
        2.2.1.1 Everyday activities
        2.2.1.2 Emotional/psychological
    2.2.2 Predictable onsets/specific ideas about 'triggers'

3. (Negative) expectations about timeline

3.1. Condition as permanent
3.2 Uncertainty over future course of illness
    3.2.1 Negative impact of ageing

4. Consequences of illness

4.1 Exclusion from participation in normal life
    4.1.1 Isolation
    4.1.2 Lack of mobility
        4.1.2.1 Weight gain
    4.1.3 Impact on social activities/life
4.2 Impact on ability to work
    4.2.1 Need for flexible work to incorporate condition
    4.2.2 Negative financial consequences of unemployment
    4.2.3 Benefits of work for condition

5. Beliefs about curability, control and management

5.1 Beliefs about curability
    5.1.1 Not curable/inevitability of condition
        5.1.1.1 Acceptance of condition
5.2 Beliefs about treatments
    5.2.1 Self-management
        5.2.1.1 Not able to self-manage/out of claimant's control
        5.2.1.2 Limiting activity/rest/fear-avoidance behaviour
        5.2.1.3 Alternative therapies

(Continued)

Figure 4.4   (Continued)

5.2.2 Medical management
    5.2.2.1 Effectiveness of treatments
    5.2.2.2 Exhausted all treatment options/'end of the road'
    5.2.2.3 Medication
        5.2.2.3.1 Need for heavy/constant pain relief
        5.2.2.3.2 Ineffectiveness/unwanted side-effects
    5.2.2.4 Surgery
    5.2.2.5 Beliefs about/experiences of management of condition
        5.2.2.5.1 GP only prescribes medication/gives long-term sick notes
        5.2.2.5.2 Dissatisfaction with healthcare/attributing blame
        5.2.2.5.3 Conferred expertise about condition/distrust of medical advice

6. Emotional representations (negative emotions reported as a consequence of condition)

6.1 Reported by SO as experienced by self
    6.1.1 Catastrophizing
    6.1.2 Anger
    6.1.3 Fear
    6.1.4 Feeling low/depressed
    6.1.5 Anxiety/worry
    6.1.6 Sadness
6.2 Reported by SO as experienced by claimant
    6.2.1 Lack of motivation
    6.2.2 Irritability
    6.2.3 Stress/worry/anxiety
    6.2.4 Feeling low/depressed
    6.2.5 Low self-esteem
6.3 Reported by claimant as experienced by SO
    6.3.1 Worry
    6.3.2 Feeling low
    6.3.3 Upset
6.4 Reported by claimant as experienced by self
    6.4.1 Stress
    6.4.2 Irritability
    6.4.3 Anxiety
    6.4.4 Anger
    6.4.5 Depression
    6.4.6 Shame
    6.4.7 Shock
    6.4.8 Catastrophizing
    6.4.9 Frustration

7. Claimant as genuine

7.1 Being 'a fighter'/stoical
    7.1.1 Not wanting to be a burden
    7.1.2 'Claimant' is not real self
7.2 Removing blame from claimant
    7.2.1 SO 'witness' to pain
    7.2.2 Claimant as a 'good patient'
    7.2.3 Wants to work but is prevented by condition

8. Impact on/influence of significant other

    8.1 Familiarity with claimant
        8.1.2 Time spent together because both not working
    8.2 Influence of SO health problems
        8.2.1 Extent of shared understanding of illness experience
        8.2.2 Negative impact on SO health
        8.2.3 Projects pessimism about own health problem
    8.3 The only carer
        8.3.1 Dedication to the claimant/routine dependency
        8.3.2 Authority on claimant's condition/protecting claimant
    8.4 Impact on SO
        8.4.1 Social life
        8.4.2 Work
    8.5 Relationship
        8.5.1 Extent of impact
        8.5.2 'Us vs rest of the world'
                8.5.1.1 Family/friends
                8.5.1.2 Benefit system
                8.5.1.3 Insurance companies
                8.5.1.4 Employer

Figure 4.4   Final version of David's template

Final interpretation and write-up

As we pointed out in the previous chapter, analysis does not end when you have constructed you final template and coded your data to it. You then face the crucial task of using your template coding to help you answer your research question(s). In David's study, he wanted to build on understandings from the mainly quantitative literature relating to illness beliefs and their impact. He therefore began this last stage of analysis by looking at how his in-depth qualitative data related to the concepts encompassed by the model. He paid particular attention to areas where his data cast new light on the model, and to those with clear implications for work participation issues. This led him to focus strongly on the themes which illustrated the inter-dependence between back pain sufferers and their significant others, and the context of the welfare system, which resulted in both parties being concerned to establish the sufferer as 'genuine'. David organized the findings section of his dissertation around the main themes, giving clear priority in terms of level of detail and subsequent depth of discussion to 'Impact on/influence of significant others' and 'Patient as genuine'. He showed how his approach extended and enriched the understanding provided by the existing mainly quantitative literature, and set his interpretation in the context of the participants' social worlds and the welfare system.

Main lessons from the analysis in this case

The example we have presented here demonstrates one way in which *a priori* themes can be usefully applied in Template Analysis. However, it is important to note that even with very 'hard' *a priori* themes, that were directly linked to the theoretical framework guiding the study, the researcher maintained an openness to his template and a willingness to modify any of his initial thematic categories. This openness also allowed David to develop and incorporate new key themes which were important to his developing understanding of potential psychosocial obstacles and the role of significant others in pain conditions. Developing a template that allowed him to code his data effectively in terms of both depth and clarity meant that David was able to combine some of his initial main themes while still exploring concepts in detail. Careful reflection during the process of template development also allowed David to design a template which could meaningfully distinguish between different participant groups, enabling him to explore his data in a way which allowed him to, for example, distinguish who was talking about whose belief or response. Using Template Analysis allowed David to readily incorporate a useful theoretical framework used primarily in quantitative work into his own qualitative exploration of a novel area. His analysis supported an existing model as a useful framework to explore beliefs about illness, but was additionally able to identify and incorporate some of the ways in which other factors and wider social circumstances may impact on work outcomes for patients with chronic back pain.

Case study 4.2   Qualitative public health project using an 'asset approach'

Background to the study

There is consensus among those responsible for promoting public health in the UK that effective community engagement is vital to achieve public health goals (e.g. NICE, 2014; Public Health England, 2015). Public health research is often based on a deficits model, with a primary focus on identifying problems and needs, and on developing services to fill gaps and fix problems. It has been suggested that this approach can lead to communities becoming disempowered and passive recipients of expensive services. There has therefore been a recent shift in UK public health policy towards an 'asset approach' (e.g. Whiting et al., 2012). While an asset approach categorically should not replace investment in improving services or tackling structural causes of inequality, the approach does differ from the more familiar deficit approach. In an assets approach, the focus is on identifying and utilizing the capacity, skills, knowledge, connections and potential available in a community as a means of empowering individuals and communities to take control of their own health and their own lives.

The researcher and their project

For our purposes here, we shall assume that this study was undertaken by Nasifah. Nasifah is studying for a Master's in Public Health Management and Organization and is, like David, required to undertake an independent research project as part of her course. Nasifah has been introduced to the assets approach as part of her studies, and she is interested in looking at how socially disadvantaged communities might identify and use 'assets' in relation to their health and well-being. It is acknowledged in the United Kingdom that, given an ageing population and tighter limits on the finances available to local government bodies, there is a need to find novel and innovative ways to deliver services for which local authority public health teams and other statutory services have previously been responsible. Nasifah's research explored ways in which community members might be able to take on some of these roles, utilizing assets readily available to them. Her project was based in a deprived city containing some of the most socially disadvantaged communities in England. For this project, she undertook focus groups with a number of successful existing community groups/organizations operating across the city. The aim of Nasifah's work was to explore, using an asset-based approach, which individual and community assets participants identified as existing in their area. Additional aims were to reflect with participants on how these assets might be utilized to improve health and well-being, and to consider how such assets might be used to promote public health as part of changes to public health provision in the context of national austerity measures and local authority budget cuts. In line with the positive perspective of the assets-based approach, Nasifah chose community groups to participate which were identified by a range of local experts in public health issues as active and successful groups.

The analysis process

Philosophical position

Nasifah chose a limited realist position for her research. She wanted to draw conclusions about the 'real' world in which her participant community groups/organizations operated, but did not feel she could step outside her subjective position in the way that a neo-positivist approach requires. One reason for this was that she had extensive experience of involvement in community organizations herself. She therefore found the constructivist epistemology of limited realism, with its emphasis on researcher reflexivity, conducive to what she wanted to achieve with the project.

Getting to know the data

Nasifah undertook focus groups with 6 diverse community initiatives, giving her a data set consisting of 6 focus group interviews all lasting around one-and-a-half hours. Nasifah was required to complete her research to very tight deadlines stipulated by her course, so in this instance it was impractical to wait until data collection was fully complete before she proceeded with analysis. Analysis therefore began after she had completed the first two focus groups, and template development and analysis proceeded in parallel with ongoing data collection. This is not uncommon in larger projects, or in projects that need to be completed within a short stipulated timeframe. However, the groups Nasifah interviewed were very diverse, and she was therefore not concerned that the data from which she created her initial template were overly homogenous. As we discussed in Chapter 3, if you do begin analysis on a subset rather than a complete body of data, it is important to ensure that you choose transcripts which represent a good cross-section of the whole data set. Failing to do this can mean that early versions of your template prove very difficult to apply to subsequent data. As Nasifah had also facilitated the focus groups, she was familiar with the content of the transcripts – she also made sure that she had read through each of the transcripts being used in initial template construction several times before moving on to preliminary coding.

Mode of analysis

Nasifah decided from the start to carry out her analysis by hand. She was aware that she had a considerable volume of complex data, and did not feel that the time it would take to learn a CAQDAS program was justified. In addition, she had some experience of hand-coding from her undergraduate degree and had found herself able to use such an approach in a careful, well-organized manner.

Use of *a priori* themes and preliminary coding

As in the previous example, Nasifah used *a priori* themes in her analysis. Like David, she drew on relevant theory to define these. In her case, her project focused on an asset-based approach to public health, and the *a priori* themes she chose were based on Morgan and Ziglio's (2007) asset-based model of health and development. This model distinguishes between assets at the *individual* level, the *community* level and the *institutional* level. Assets at the individual level include social competence; resistance skills; commitment to learning; positive values; self-esteem; a sense of purpose. Assets at the community level include family and friendship (supportive) networks; intergenerational solidarity; community cohesion; affinity groups (mutual aid); and religious tolerance. Assets at the institutional level include environmental resources; employment security; voluntary service opportunities; safe housing; political democracy and participation opportunities; social justice and equity. Nasifah therefore identified three *a priori* themes – (1) individual assets, (2) community assets and (3) institutional assets – to use in the formulation of the initial coding template. Note that these are much broader than those used by David, and as such can be seen as 'soft' rather than 'hard' *a priori* themes (see page 29). This is in keeping with her limited realist approach, which tends to be less likely than neo-positivist research to impose a detailed theoretical framework on the analysis.

Formulating the initial template

Nasifah began template formulation having undertaken preliminary coding on two focus group transcripts. Having gone through both transcripts identifying initial themes, she then roughly grouped themes under the three *a priori* headings of individual, community and institutional assets. Nasifah used colour coded Post-it notes to distinguish between the three headings – any themes relating to 'individual assets' were written on yellow Post-it notes; themes relating to 'community assets' written on orange Post-it notes; and themes relating to 'organizational assets' on pink Post-it notes. Any themes which appeared to relate to more than one heading were duplicated – they were written out the required number of times on the relevant colour Post-it note – and marked with an asterisk.

This process resulted in three distinct colour coded piles (pink, yellow and orange) relating to her three broad *a priori* themes. Nasifah then took some time to look through the themes in each pile to consider carefully how they should be appropriately grouped. At this stage she also carried out independent coding quality checks, asking a colleague to identify their own preliminary themes from the same two focus group transcripts and to see if they felt they would 'fit' under the three *a priori* top-level themes. Discussion of similarities and differences between coders led to some reorganization, renaming and a change of focus (rather than starting with the individual and moving outwards to the wider context, Nasifah decided rather to start with wider societal themes with a progressive focus into the area of more individual assets).

The culmination of this work was six top-level thematic category headings – Table 4.1 shows these top-level themes and clarifies how these were derived from the original three *a priori* themes.

Table 4.1 Developing Nasifah's top-level themes

Top-level theme	Initial a priori theme
1 Societal factors What are the wider societal factors?	Derived from original *institutional assets* theme
2 Professional roles What is the best role for professionals?	Derived from original *institutional assets* theme
3 Relations with other groups and communities How do participants relate to the local area and other local communities/groups?	Derived from original *institutional* and *community assets* themes
4 Immediate community assets What assets are identified in relation to the immediate local community?	Derived from original *community assets* theme
5 Group characteristics What assets are identified as deriving from the group themselves?	Derived from original *community assets* theme
6 Personal/individual assets and benefits What personal assets do individual group members bring?	Derived from original *individual assets* theme

Nasifah then compiled these into a document which formed her initial template – this document (see Table 4.2) delineated each top-level theme and listed the type of sub-themes she expected to cover in this category based on both her initial

Table 4.2 Developing Nasifah's initial template – defining thematic categories

Main theme	Defining scope of theme
1 Societal factors What are the wider societal factors?	This theme refers to wider national issues which are identified as having an important impact in local terms but are not really seen as being amenable to change at local level. Sub-themes should cover: *Value to society* Includes: hidden savings (members of community groups less likely to be costing statutory services money); value for money – operate at much less cost than statutory services as well as being affordable for members (aware of extent of personal financial constraints of members of local community). *National policy* Includes: funding issues – lack of stability (pot available one year has disappeared the next); restrictions on who can apply for what – more support for smaller local groups unable to meet charitable status required; time-consuming nature of seeking out funding. *Set-up time* The importance of the initial set-up period often emphasized (allowing sufficient time to embed and develop) and often policy initiatives and changes not felt to support this. *North–south divide (in UK)* Poor reputation, isolation – but also the potential benefits of these!

Main theme	Defining scope of theme
2 Professional roles What is the best role for professionals?	Sub-themes should cover: *The advantages of community initiatives* Professionals only work 9–5 (community members/groups more flexible – and needs don't only arise 9–5); lack of stability in relation to professionals – posts disappearing or changing, individuals leaving – community members more 'stable'. *Ways in which professionals can help community projects* Important role in supporting initial set-up of community initiatives (note help in transferring ownership to community members – formal constitution, etc.) – previous Community Development Worker role appreciated – no longer exists; money issues (funding source/identification of funding sources – also, holding purse strings for limited time). *Recognizing and validating community initiatives* Provision of formal training (helps networking, especially making connections with other community groups); referring into project/publicizing project; (voluntary) participation in supporting project in professional role; formal awards recognizing project.
3 Relations with other groups and communities How do participants relate to other local communities/ groups?	Sub-themes should cover: *Issues around venues* Safety and accessibility; issues relating to venue hire. *Training and events facilitating networking with other groups* *Providing peer support to help set up similar initiatives elsewhere in the city* *Extent of contact and interaction with other groups* Sometimes excellent, sometimes not, e.g. various loaded comments that other groups may be 'using' or 'taking credit' for own work.
4 Immediate community assets What assets are identified in relation to the immediate local community?	Sub-themes should cover: *Reputations and reality* The local area (what's distinctive, what's good and what's bad about the city and the people who live there). *Reputations in relation to the group specifically* Groups work hard to establish a good reputation; word of mouth of key importance in establishing and maintaining successful community initiatives. *The role of community group members as ambassadors* Both for the city and their particular community group. *Our role as community experts* As members of their local community, sense that participants understand better what their community wants/needs than professionals; as members of community, better placed/better able

(Continued)

Table 4.2   (Continued)

Main theme	Defining scope of theme
	to access some 'hard to reach' groups than professionals (sometimes this is due to a more receptive response to volunteers than services).
	Experts in the community Able to provide a bridge/link between professionals/services and the community.
5 Group characteristics What assets are identified as deriving from the group themselves?	Sub-themes should cover: *Groups are run on principles of democratic consensus* *Groups identify themselves as inclusive* But note there are some tensions here – if so close knit, might it be difficult for newcomers? *Strong group identity* *Members feel they have ownership of their group* Paying reasonable subs helps this sense. *Groups founded on a core 'issue'* 'Founding principle' which remains of importance to the entire membership. *Groups broaden focus over time* Despite above point, groups do become more holistic (incorporate other 'issues'/activities) and develop/change – balance between flexibility and stability. *Importance of social interaction* Social events are an important part – integral and needed, not an 'extra' – both to form strong bonds as group and reward efforts. *Group leadership and core membership* Usually a strong core committed group willing to take on responsibilities and with popular charismatic leadership – with a wider more rotating membership. *Group resilience* Celebrate their successes, they know their purpose and their limitations, they rationalize and do not dwell on 'failures'.
6 Personal/individual assets and benefits What personal assets do individual group members bring?	Sub-themes include: *Physical and mental health are interlinked and equally important* *Group participation is personally rewarding* Health benefits, psychological benefits. *Glad to be helping others* … but explicit that this improves own well-being too! *Recognition and acknowledgement is rewarding* Media coverage is particularly popular; having personal experience recognized as expertise.

Main theme	Defining scope of theme
	Personal development Training, education (most valued when recognized with a qualification/ certificate).
	Social benefits A number of groups include participants who, without it, are at high risk of social isolation.
	Requires time and commitment

coding of the first two transcripts as well as drawing on the known content of other focus groups she had completed as data collection continued. This document was then transformed into an initial template, with the sub-themes identified, numbered and appropriately hierarchically ordered.

Developing and applying the template

Once Nasifah had developed an initial template, she then applied this to a new transcript from her third focus group. Rather than using paper and Post-it notes, on this occasion coding was undertaken using word-processing software (Microsoft Word). Nasifah had two documents open simultaneously on her desktop computer: the focus group transcript and a copy of the initial template. She read carefully through the transcript and used the 'copy' and 'paste' functions to paste any relevant segments of talk from the transcript under the relevant section on the template. The comment function was used to label each segment with the appropriate transcript line number so it would not be problematic to locate in the future. Nasifah also kept a 'clean version' template (without quotes) to refer back to, and used the 'track changes' function to keep a record of how the template was developing. Once she had gone through the transcript in full, Nasifah returned to the template and considered where she felt it necessary to think about developing her coding, especially in terms of its depth. In this particular project, Nasifah did not find it necessary to make substantial changes to her six top-level themes. Her task was rather to ensure that the sub-themes under each heading were fully developed, described and delineated so that they incorporated all relevant information. She continued to add new themes as appropriate and increase the depth of her coding as she worked her way through the entire body of data. Figure 4.5 provides an example of how coding developed for one of the top-level hierarchical themes: 'Ways in which professionals can help community projects' and shows how both the number of themes both at higher and sub-level encompassed under this heading increased as analysis progressed.

From template version 2:

2.2 Ways in which professionals can help community projects

2.2.1 Important role in supporting initial set up of community initiatives
2.2.2 Money issues
2.2.3 Recognizing and validating
    2.2.3.1 Provision of formal training
    2.2.3.2 Referring into project/publicizing project
    2.2.3.3 (Voluntary) participation in supporting project in professional role
    2.2.3.4 Formal awards recognizing project

From template version 3:

2.2 Ways in which professionals can help community projects

2.2.1 Important role in supporting initial set up of community initiatives
2.2.2 Funding issues
2.2.3 Recognizing and validating
    2.2.3.1 Provision of formal training
    2.2.3.2 Referring into project/publicizing project
    2.2.3.3 (Voluntary) participation in supporting project in professional role
    2.2.3.4 Formal awards recognizing project
2.2.4 Salaried employees and community projects
2.2.5 Providing and facilitating a central information point

From final version template (template version 6):

2.2 Ways in which professionals can help community projects

2.2.1 Important role in supporting initial set up of community initiatives
    2.2.1.1 Willing to support the innovative
        2.2.1.1.1 Assistance in transfer of ownership, formalizing constitution, etc.
        2.2.1.1.2 Holding the purse strings for initial period
2.2.2 Funding issues
    2.2.2.1 Providing a source of funding
    2.2.2.2 Assistance in identifying appropriate sources of funding
2.2.3 Recognizing and validating
    2.2.3.1 Provision of formal training
        2.2.3.1.1 How this helps networking – making connections with other community groups
    2.2.3.2 Referring into project/publicizing project
    2.2.3.3 (Voluntary) participation in supporting project in professional role
    2.2.3.4 Formal awards recognizing project
2.2.4 Facilitating communication centrally
    2.2.4.1 Existing
    2.2.4.2 Planned
    2.2.4.3 Wanted
2.2.5 'Let it go' – allowing sufficient autonomy and flexibility

---

Figure 4.5 Developing depth of coding for one of Nasifah's top-level themes

Throughout the analysis, Nasifah obtained critical feedback from her supervisor on her developing template. She also kept a reflective diary from the start of the project, enabling her to consider reflexively her own position in relation to the research. Consideration of 'quality' in her analysis was therefore not simply a matter of the formal independent rater comparison mentioned earlier; rather it was an ongoing process that continued to the point of write-up. This is in keeping with the limited realist position she took, as discussed in Chapter 2.

Final interpretation and write-up

Nasifah was interested in her study in identifying key assets of different types and at different levels that enabled community groups to contribute positively to health and well-being. At the same time, she needed to know what difficulties the groups may have faced in doing this. She looked at the coding in relation to each group individually to construct a story of how it functioned, and what factors enabled or impeded its success. Looking across all the cases, it was clear that despite considerable variation, those assets identified through main theme 5 (Group characteristics – What assets are identified as deriving from the group themselves?) needed to be at the heart of her interpretation. She therefore wrote case studies of each of the groups which examined how wider context at varying levels (main themes 1 to 4, see Table 4.2) shaped the way groups were able to function, and how this in turn related to members as providers of individual/personal assets (main theme 6).

For her write-up, Nasifah felt it was important to give a rounded sense of how the activities of particular groups could be understood in terms of different types of assets. She therefore presented three case studies of very different groups, highlighting prominent themes within each of them. This was followed by an overview of key findings in relation to each top-level theme across all the groups.

Nasifah's final template

Towards the end of her project, Nasifah gave a presentation on emerging findings to representatives from participating groups, and facilitated a discussion afterwards. This not only served dissemination purposes but also acted as a further chance to reflect on the template before it was finalized for her dissertation. Nasifah's final coding template (see Figure 4.6) was comprised of six top-level hierarchical themes which are in essence those she decided upon when formulating her initial template (see Table 4.2), although she did alter the wording of some headings slightly to ensure these were better representative of the data and her findings. She then revisited the data set and analysed each transcript using the final version template. The template was then used as a guiding framework to produce a full research report.

1. What is the wider societal context/issues?

1.1 Value to society

    1.1.1   Hidden savings
    1.1.2   Value for money
        1.1.2.1   Operate at much less cost
        1.1.2.2   Affordable for members

1.2 Funders and funding

    1.2.1   Funding issues
        1.2.1.1   Continuity problems
            1.2.1.1.1   Lack of stability
            1.2.1.1.2   Limited period funding
            1.2.1.1.3   Funding limited to new
        1.2.1.2   Restrictions
            1.2.1.2.1   Who can apply for what
            1.2.1.2.2   What money spent on
            1.2.1.2.3   Associated bureaucracy
    1.2.2   Time issues
        1.2.2.1   Initial set up period
        1.2.2.2   Funding existing vs new

1.3 Wider social context

    1.3.1   Unemployment
    1.3.2   North–south divide
    1.3.3   Austerity measures
        1.3.3.1   Ruthlessness

2. What is the best role for outside professionals?

2.1 The advantages of community initiatives

    2.1.1   Professionals only work 9–5
    2.1.2   Lack of stability in relation to professionals
        2.1.2.1   Posts disappearing or changing
        2.1.2.2   Individuals leaving
    2.1.3   Extent of group autonomy and independence

2.2 Ways in which professionals can help community projects

    2.2.1   Role in supporting initial set up
        2.2.1.1   Supporting innovation
            2.2.1.1.1   Assistance in transfer of ownership, formalizing constitution, etc.
            2.2.1.1.2   Holding the purse strings
    2.2.2   Funding issues
        2.2.2.1   Providing
        2.2.2.2   Assistance in identifying
    2.2.3   Recognizing and validating
        2.2.3.1   Provision of training
            2.2.3.1.1   Networking
        2.2.3.2   Using the project
        2.2.3.3   Participation
        2.2.3.4   Formal awards

2.2.4 Facilitating communication centrally
    2.2.4.1 Existing
    2.2.4.2 Planned
    2.2.4.3 Wanted
2.2.5 'Let it go' – allowing sufficient autonomy and flexibility

3. How do participants relate to other local communities/groups?

3.1 Issues around venues
3.2 Training and events
3.3 Providing peer support
3.4 Contact and interaction

3.4.1 External/other services that facilitate recruitment
    3.4.1.1 Social media
3.4.2 Where there are problems
    3.4.2.1 'Other' (BME)
    3.4.2.2 'Using' or 'taking credit'
3.4.3 Direct involvement of other groups
3.4.4 Quality of communication

3.5 Previous experience of groups
3.6 Groups outside city

4. What assets are identified in relation to own (local) community?

4.1 Reputations and reality

4.1.1 The city
    4.1.1.1 Changes in recent years
    4.1.1.2 City's external reputation
4.1.2 The local area
    4.1.2.1 Established communities
    4.1.2.2 Changes
        4.1.2.2.1 Eastern European
    4.1.2.3 Made up of 'good people'
    4.1.2.4 Specific areas

4.2 Group's reputation

4.2.1 'Word of mouth'
4.2.2 Ambassador role

4.3 Our role as community experts

4.3.1 Understand what is wanted/needed
    4.3.1.1 Responsiveness
    4.3.1.2 Non-judgemental
4.3.2 Better able to access 'hard to reach'
4.3.3 Providing a bridge between professionals and community
4.3.4 Flexibility
    4.3.4.1 A different ethos
        4.3.4.1.1 Individualized
4.3.5 Filling gaps

(Continued)

Figure 4.6   (Continued)

4.4   Why our community needs this group

    4.4.1   For the future generation
    4.4.2   Group strengthens the community

4.5   Looking after your own

    4.5.1   Helping to look after themselves

5.   Group characteristics – What assets are identified as deriving from the group themselves?

5.1   How groups are run

    5.1.1   Democratic consensus
    5.1.2   Groups identify themselves as inclusive
    5.1.3   Leadership
        5.1.3.1   Paid employees leading
        5.1.3.2   Charismatic leadership
        5.1.3.3   A strong core
        5.1.3.4   Responsibilities
            5.1.3.4.1   Ownership of group
            5.1.3.4.2   Own patch/activity

5.2   Remit of group

    5.2.1   Founded on a core 'issue'
    5.2.2   Becoming more holistic
    5.2.3   Role of social events
    5.2.4   Group entrepreneurial activities

5.3   Resilience

6.   Personal/individual assets and benefits

6.1   Health

    6.1.1   Physical and mental health interlinked
    6.1.2   Personally rewarding
        6.1.2.1   Physical health benefits
        6.1.2.2   Psychological benefits

6.2   Members' skills and experience

    6.2.1   Recognition and acknowledgement
    6.2.2   Having personal experience recognized as expertise
    6.2.3   Personal development

6.3   Social

    6.3.1   Glad to be helping others …
        6.3.1.1   But explicit that this improves own well-being too!

> 6.3.2 Social benefits (a number of groups involve participants who, without it, are at high risk of social isolation)
>
> **6.4 Volunteering**
>
> 6.4.1 Requires time and commitment
> 6.4.1.1 Competing demands on volunteer time
> 6.4.2 But it is a choice, my choice – voluntary, not forced – focus is on adding something to my life not negative messages (compared with stop smoking messages)
> 6.4.3 Links to paid employment
> 6.4.3.1 Provides skills necessary
> 6.4.4 Status of volunteers – tensions between professional and volunteer identities

Figure 4.6   Nasifah's final template

Main lessons from the analysis in this case

This example shows the potential value of using broad *a priori* themes. Nasifah was able to use the three top-level themes to focus her analysis around issues in the theoretical and practice/policy literature, but also to allow detailed 'bottom-up' coding within the broad themes that was well grounded in participants' experiences. Coding in depth enabled Nasifah to investigate in real detail the different assets available to different communities in the research setting, revealing where there were commonalities and where there were differences, as well as exploring how these assets might be utilized to improve health and well-being more widely.

This project also provides an example of how practical concerns and limitations may impact upon the way you undertake analysis. In this case study, it was necessary to commence analysis prior to the completion of data collection as, given the time constraints Nasifah was committed to, it would have been impractical to wait until all data were collected in order to read through the full data set before commencing analysis. However, it was important to ensure that earlier transcripts were not overly homogeneous to ensure that early versions of her template were not difficult to apply to subsequent data – in this particular project, this did not prove problematic as the community groups Nasifah was interviewing were selected to cover a diverse range of types. As Nasifah was responsible for undertaking both data collection and analysis in this project, she was usefully able to draw on her familiarity and understanding of the data set as a whole while she proceeded with template development.

CHAPTER SUMMARY

In this chapter we have provided two fictionalized case studies based on examples from our own research which we hope have demonstrated how Template Analysis can be usefully applied in different types of research project (for more worked examples, see Brooks et al., 2015). In presenting these examples, we have highlighted particular challenges that the 'students' faced, and how they addressed them. We recognize, though, that any after-the-fact narrative tends to make the research process look more linear and tidy than it actually is. An important learning point is that the reality of analysis is always messier than any textbook account, and that you should be prepared for this and not let it undermine your confidence. Being well organized and keeping a good record of your analytical choices at each step can be very helpful to prevent messiness descending into chaos.

We hope that these examples mean that you now feel well able to undertake Template Analysis on your own data and are all set to undertake your own piece of research. In the following chapter, we'll take a look at how Template Analysis has been used in published literature by researchers working in this field.

5

THE USE OF TEMPLATE ANALYSIS IN PUBLISHED RESEARCH: THE CAREERS LITERATURE AS AN EXEMPLAR

In the previous chapter, we looked in detail at two fictionalized examples of studies using Template Analysis, based on our own research. These were both located in the intersection between organizational and health/well-being research, where much of our own research is focused. The aim of the present chapter is to widen the range of examples, to help you think about the decisions you will have to make in using Template Analysis in your own project. Our initial thought was to review a selection of articles about studies with varied settings, topics and designs. It soon became apparent, however, that there were problems with this strategy. The sheer number and variety of studies using our technique made it difficult to select a sample of them that could usefully illustrate analytical choices – there was a danger we would just be comparing 'chalk and cheese' with little for you as a reader to draw from it. We therefore decided to review studies within one broad area of business and management research where Template Analysis has been used frequently. After much deliberation, we settled on the careers literature as our exemplar. Not only is there a good range of articles incorporating Template Analysis in this area, it is also sufficiently diverse to raise an interesting range of challenges while coherent enough to enable fruitful comparisons.

To best illustrate the ways in which authors working in this area have used Template Analysis, we have selected six key articles to discuss in some depth. We have picked these because they all provide a reasonable amount of detail about how they used Template Analysis, while differing in precise topic area, research design and philosophical/theoretical position. Three of the six articles describe research carried out in non-European settings, specifically a major South East Asian city (Dickmann and Cerdin, 2014), Sri Lanka (Fernando and Cohen, 2011) and New Zealand (Lips-Wiersma and Hall, 2007). They are also all interesting papers in their own right. The chosen articles are:

Dickmann, M. and Cerdin, J.L. (2014) Boundaryless career drivers: exploring macro-contextual factors in location decisions. *Journal of Global Mobility*, 2 (1): 26–52.

Focusing on one South East Asian city, the authors conducted interviews with those who had moved to the city from abroad, had been born in the city and remained there, or had moved from the city to a foreign location (total n = 43). Their analysis highlights macro-contextual factors – such things as qualities of the environment, personal freedom and economic growth – that influenced career location decisions.

Fernando, W.D.A. and Cohen, L. (2011) Exploring the interplay between gender, organizational context and career: a Sri Lankan perspective. *Career Development International*, 16 (6): 553–571.

The authors interviewed 24 Sri Lankan women at different points in their careers to examine how they navigated the opportunities and constraints in their organizational contexts in order to achieve hierarchical advancement. Using a social constructionist approach, they highlight eight different 'modes of engagement' used by the women, and discuss the pervasive impact of gender expectations.

Kidd, J.M. (2008) Exploring the components of career well-being and the emotions associated with significant career experiences. *Journal of Career Development*, 35 (2): 166–186.

This study collected data from a varied sample of 89 people via a qualitative questionnaire, asking them about instances in which they had felt particularly positive or negative about their careers. Analysis showed that career transitions were a particularly important focus of strong emotional experiences, both positive and negative. Interpersonal difficulties were commonly presented as leading to significant negative emotions.

Lips-Wiersma, M. and Hall, D.T. (2007) Organizational career development is not dead: a case study on managing the new career during organizational change. *Journal of Organizational Behavior*, 28(6): 771–792.

Using a case study of a single organization, the authors explored whether and how individuals took greater responsibility for their careers at times of organizational change. They conducted 50 interviews with a wide cross-section of employees. Their analysis showed that individuals did appear to respond to change by taking greater responsibility for their own career development. At the same time, the organization itself was actively involved in career management, but this did not take the form of a traditional top-down strategy. Instead they describe a highly interactive process between individual and organization which they characterize as a kind of 'dance'.

Mallon, M. and Cohen, L. (2001) Time for a change? Women's accounts of the move from organizational careers to self-employment. *British Journal of Management*, 12: 217–230.

In this study, the authors explored how women accounted for their choice to move from organizational careers to self-employment. Data were collected through interviews with 41 women who had moved to self-employment from middle or senior managerial or professional positions. On the basis of their analysis, the authors categorized the women in two broad groups in terms of their stated motives for change: those who were 'entrepreneurs-in-waiting' and those whose choice reflected dissatisfaction and disillusionment with the organization. However, this distinction was not entirely clear-cut and there was considerable differentiation within categories. Further analysis identified three themes that permeated accounts across categories: 'organizational life', 'values and integrity' and '(im)balance between personal and professional life'.

Wyatt, M. and Silvester, J. (2015) Reflections on the labyrinth: investigating black and minority ethnic leaders' career experiences. *Human Relations*, 68 (8): 1243–1269.

Drawing on attribution theory, this study examined how 20 black and ethnic minority (BME) and 20 white leaders made sense of significant incidents in their careers. There were four common themes identified by both groups as important in how they negotiated their career journeys: 'visibility', 'networks', 'development' and 'line manager support'. However, BME leaders described greater difficulties than white leaders in utilizing informal networks and therefore placed greater reliance on formal procedures to advance their careers.

In addition to these examples, we will make reference to a range of other articles on aspects of careers, to help illustrate the main points we highlight. We have organized our consideration of this literature around four issues: the *philosophical approach* taken (referring to our classification suggested in Chapter 2); the *method of data collection*; how and why *a priori themes* are used (if at all); how issues of the *quality of analysis* are addressed. Table 5.1 summarizes the position of our selected articles on each of these issues.

Table 5.1 Details of main articles included in the review

Article	Philosophical approach	Data collection method(s)	Use of a priori themes	Quality assurance
Dickmann, M. and Cerdin, J.L. (2014) Boundaryless career drivers – exploring macro-contextual factors in location decisions. *Journal of Global Mobility*, 2 (1): 26–52.	Not stated. Implicitly realist – on boundary of neo-positivist and limited realist approaches.	Semi-structured interviews, either face-to-face (n = 31) or by telephone (n = 12). Duration 45 minutes to 2 hours.	Yes, based on literature.	Two researchers carried out analysis together. Differences in coding between them discussed. Original interviewees approached for clarifications in coding.
Fernando, W.D.A. and Cohen, L. (2011) Exploring the interplay between gender, organizational context and career: a Sri Lankan perspective. *Career Development International*, 16 (6): 553–571.	Social constructionist – some aspects of contextual constructivism, some radical constructionism.	Face-to-face interviews with 24 women in private and public organizations in Sri Lanka. Written notes taken as respondents concerned about potential identifiability of audio files.	Yes, based on literature and personal experience of first researcher.	Careful reading of data and incremental development of themes by two researchers. Focus on contrasting and minority positions. Extensive iterative modification of template. Emphasis on retaining grasp of 'big picture'. N.B. in keeping with social constructionist approach, no use of inter-rater agreement.
Kidd, J.M. (2008) Exploring the components of career well-being and the emotions associated with significant career experiences. *Journal of Career Development*, 35 (2): 166–186.	Not stated. Implicitly realist – closer to neo-positivist than limited realist. Treats emotion examples as objective 'facts', uses inter-rater agreement, etc.	Qualitative questionnaire e-mailed to part-time students with varied career histories (n=89).	No mention – appear not to have been used.	Inter-rater agreement at two stages, with two different colleagues. Percentage agreement quoted for second check (74%). Disagreements resolved by mutual consultation.

Article	Philosophical approach	Data collection method(s)	Use of a priori themes	Quality assurance
Lips-Wiersma, M. and Hall, D.T. (2007) Organizational career development is not dead: a case study on managing the new career during organizational change. *Journal of Organizational Behavior*, 28(6): 771–792.	Not stated, other than 'in-depth, qualitative, instrumental case study'. Implicitly realist – in grey area between neo-positivist and limited realist.	Semi-structured interviews with 50 research participants; representative sample from eight work units of one organization.	Two main *a priori* codes used – drawn (loosely) from the literature.	Two researchers developed template and coded together. Five transcripts coded to final template by 12 postgraduate students, independent of the researchers. Lincoln and Guba (1985) criteria addressed.
Mallon, M. and Cohen, L. (2001) Time for a change? Women's accounts of the move from organizational careers to self-employment. *British Journal of Management*, 12: 217–230.	Described as rooted in life history methodology. Concerned with discourses but also presents findings some of the time in more experiential manner. Clearly constructionist – includes elements of contextualism and radical constructionism.	Semi-structured face-to-face interviews with 41 professional and managerial women who had moved from organizational to self-employment.	Not explicitly stated. Implication of some *a priori* aspects to analysis but no reference to specific *a priori* themes.	Discussion of thorough and systematic analysis, but no explicit consideration of quality of analysis.
Wyatt, M. and Silvester, J. (2015) Reflections on the labyrinth: investigating black and minority ethnic leaders' career experiences. *Human Relations*, 68 (8): 1243–1269.	Not stated. Implicitly realist. Some features typical of limited realism – e.g. explicit use of reflexivity.	Semi-structured interviews with 20 BME and 20 white senior managers from UK government department, including Critical Incident Technique.	Yes – developed from literature. N.B. separate templates developed for BME and white participants. *A priori* themes informed the first (BME) template; this in turn was used as starting point for white template.	Emphasizes reflexivity of researchers. Independent BME colleague also coded. Final templates checked with sub-sample of participants – minor modification noted.

PHILOSOPHICAL APPROACH

It is striking how rarely the articles we looked at – both our selected examples and in the wider careers literature – explicitly stated their philosophical position. In fact it is primarily those few authors who took some form of social constructionist approach that made clear reference to their philosophical assumptions (e.g. Mallon and Cohen, 2001; Fernando and Cohen, 2011; Clarke and Knights, 2015). This seems to reflect the fact that they wished to promote their approach as a contrast to that evident in most of the existing careers literature (e.g. Cohen et al., 2004). Our wider reading of articles using Template Analysis in the business and management literature suggests the limited attention to philosophical position is not in any way peculiar to the careers area.

To locate most articles within the range of philosophical positions we described in Chapter 2, we needed to make our own judgement, based on such things as the rationale given for the overall design and/or the method of data analysis, the type of quality check employed, and the claims made (if any) in relation to prior theory. On the basis of this, we would define most of the published studies as being at the realist end of the spectrum – including four of our six exemplar articles – since they stated or strongly implied they were concerned with a 'real' world that existed outside the research process. Often, though, it was not easy to make a more precise distinction as to whether the approach in a particular study was best seen as qualitative neo-positivist or limited realist. Sometimes we felt that authors had simply not had the word space within their journal's limits to clarify their assumptions, but more often there appeared to be a lack of clarity as to epistemological position.

One might argue that the blurring of philosophical positions is not in itself problematic; after all we made the point in Chapter 2 that the positions we outlined are most accurately thought of as being on a spectrum rather than as distinct and separate categories. We can see this also in the two non-realist articles included in Table 5.1: Fernando and Cohen (2011) and Mallon and Cohen (2001). Although these address their philosophical commitments much more explicitly than the other (realist) articles, in both cases they may be seen as occupying something of a grey area between contextualist and radical constructionist approaches. For example, both are concerned with 'discourses' but at the same time present much of their findings as much in terms of the quality of personal experience as discursive strategies. We would argue that there is a difference between studies that articulate a philosophical position that is genuinely and legitimately on the boundary between the categories we have outlined, and those which are unclear, contradictory or simply silent as to their position.

Thinking about your own work, you might consider that the lack of explicit attention to philosophical position in published articles – some in high-ranking journals – means you do not really need to concern yourself with this issue in your thesis. We would warn you against such a conclusion, for two reasons. Firstly, the expectations of a Master's thesis are different from those of a journal article. While for the latter, a journal editor is most concerned with the value of a submitted article's contribution to knowledge, and will take on trust the author's research competence (unless anything points to the contrary), a thesis examiner will expect to see you justify all your decisions about your research approach and design. Being clear about your philosophical position, and working it through in terms of the implementation of your research design, will certainly be seen positively. Secondly, we feel that with growing awareness of the variety of qualitative methods, the willingness of journal editors to accept an unelaborated 'garden variety' realism is diminishing. As you may well want to publish your Master's research, and may want to go further in an academic career, thinking through your philosophical position is a good habit to get in to!

DATA COLLECTION METHOD

Unsurprisingly, in terms of data collection methods, the careers literature utilizing Template Analysis is dominated by face-to-face semi-structured interviews. Five of our six selected key articles used the method, as did the clear majority of other published studies we looked at. This reflects the situation in qualitative research generally (King and Horrocks, 2010), including the whole range of qualitative business and management research (Myers, 2013). However, among the studies we have reviewed, there are plenty using methods other than interviews. Among our key articles, Kidd (2008) used an open-ended questionnaire (as we noted in Chapter 1). Looking more widely, Point and Dickmann (2012) analysed the content of international companies' web pages, with respect to how they represented issues of international mobility and global career development. Several articles described mixed methods studies – either presenting both quantitative and qualitative analyses side-by-side (e.g. Brooks and Youngson, 2014) or publishing the qualitative arm of the study separately from the quantitative (e.g. Zikic and Richardson, 2007). It is clear that Template Analysis can work perfectly well with forms of data other than the conventional interview transcript.

Even within interview-based studies, there is variety in the form the method takes. For example, Dickmann and Cerdin (2014), in their study of location choices in 'boundaryless' careers, used telephone interviews as well as face-to-face for practical reasons. Wyatt and Silvester (2015) incorporated a visual career 'timeline' tool to facilitate their interviews with BME leaders, and also used a Critical Incident Technique within the interview design. We would encourage you to think creatively about whether and how to use interviews in your own research.

USE OF *A PRIORI* THEMES

A clear majority of the articles we read were explicit that they used *a priori* themes within their analysis. Most commonly, these were drawn from previous literature, though quite often authors did not actually state what their a priori themes were. Studies differ in whether their *a priori* themes were strongly and directly linked to prior theory, or were more loosely derived from issues apparent in the literature; this represents the contrast between relatively 'hard' and 'soft' *a priori* themes that we discussed in Chapter 3. For example, Dickmann and Cerdin (2014) list a series of *a priori* themes derived directly from Van Assen et al.'s (2008) PESTEL[1] framework in the context of the literature on career decisions. These can be seen as relatively 'hard' *a priori* themes. Similarly, Vaag et al. (2014) drew *a priori* themes directly from the demand and resources model (Bakker and Demrouti, 2007) in their study of the careers of Norwegian freelance musicians. In contrast, Lips-Wiersma and Hall (2007) used two very broad *a priori* themes – 'individual responsibility' and 'organizational responsibility' – in their study of career management in times of organizational change. These may be seen as relatively 'soft' *a priori* themes.

In some studies, sources other than (or in addition to) previous literature/theory were drawn on to inform *a priori* themes. For instance, Fernando and Cohen (2011) drew on the first author's personal experience of the Sri Lankan organizational context in examining the notion of 'respectability femininity' in women's careers in that country. Wyatt and Silvester (2015) drew on the template they developed from the accounts of BME managers to inform the development of a separate template for white managers.

Using *a priori* themes is not compulsory in Template Analysis, but it is very common, as is illustrated in the example of the careers literature. We were pleased to see that many of the articles we read gave some detail of how they used *a priori* themes, and looking at how they are used in published research can be helpful to guide your own analytical strategy. But as with the issue of philosophical position, for a thesis that will be subject to examination you need to provide more detail about your use of *a priori* themes than is possible in a journal article. We would suggest you need to state which themes were defined *a priori*, to justify why you used them at all, and clarify whether they were relatively 'hard' or 'soft' in style. In discussing the development of your thesis it is particularly important to explain any changes you made to your *a priori* themes, including decisions to remove them altogether – for example, were they merged with other themes, redefined or simply deleted because they did not prove to be relevant?

---

[1] PESTEL stands for Political, Economic, Social, Technological, Ecological and Legal factors.

QUALITY OF ANALYSIS

The majority of articles, including all six of our selected key examples, gave some attention to the issue of quality of analysis, whether by highlighting the thorough and systematic way they carried it out, or by describing specific quality checks (or both). They differed quite considerably, though, in the amount of detail they provided, as can be seen in Table 5.1 for the key articles. By far the most common specific check was the use of some form of comparison between independent coders. Studies varied in who was involved in the independent coding, including comparisons within the research team (e.g. Dickmann and Cerdin, 2014), between the research team and independent academic colleagues (e.g. Kidd, 2008), and with the research participants themselves (e.g. Wyatt and Silvester, 2015). In line with explicit or implicit philosophical positions, they also varied in how the comparisons were used. Those which could be seen as including elements of neo-positivism were more likely to present the exercise as one of 'validation' of themes; for instance, Kidd (2008) calculated percentage agreements between coders. Those more clearly in the limited realist camp tended to frame the task in terms of stimulating critical thinking on the part of the researchers and/or increasing the transparency of coding decisions (e.g. Lips-Wiersma and Hall, 2007; Vaag et al., 2014). Studies using a social constructionist approach were least likely to use a formal inter-coder comparison, but did emphasize a rigorous and critical approach to analysis (e.g. Mallon and Cohen, 2001; Clarke and Knights, 2015).

We were struck by how few articles discussed reflexivity in their accounts of their analysis and the conclusions they drew from it. Clarke and Knights (2015) do consider their own position as academics in Business Schools considering the career accounts of their peers, and Wyatt and Silvester (2015) showed reflexive awareness of ethnicity in their analysis of BME managers' interviews; these articles were in a clear minority. The absence of reflexivity is surprising given its importance is emphasized in most qualitative textbooks, including in business and management research (e.g. Haynes, 2012; Bell and Thorpe, 2013) and is intrinsic to all the philosophical approaches we have described, arguably excepting qualitative neo-positivism. Of course, the fact that reflexivity is not discussed in most articles does not necessarily mean that it was not considered by researchers; at least in some cases the expectations of journals may have led to authors not addressing it or even to it being removed on review.

To further illustrate how analytical quality may be addressed in Template Analysis, we will describe in some detail the approach taken in three of our selected key articles. Lips-Wiersma and Hall's (2007) study of career development in the context of organizational change addressed quality in a number of ways. They describe thorough reading of the text by both researchers in order to develop the final template. They then asked 12 postgraduate students enrolled on a qualitative methods course to check that the template was 'sufficiently comprehensive' by applying it to five (out of 50) randomly chosen transcripts. At the end of the study they sought feedback from participants on their findings. These specific activities were set in an overall approach to quality guided by Lincoln and Guba's (1985) four criteria of trustworthiness in qualitative analysis: credibility, transferability, dependability and confirmability. They explain their strategy as follows:

> Their criteria of credibility were met in this study through prolonged engagement in the field, feedback by research participants on the final results, and ongoing peer debriefing. Their criterion of transferability was met by a detailed (thick) description of the organizational context. Their criteria of dependability were met by protecting participants' confidentiality and drawing on a soundly justified and significant (for qualitative research) sample. Their criteria of confirmability were met by using the well-established method of template analysis, meticulous data management through use of Nu.dist, the use of 'outsiders' to confirm our template, and transparent presentation of the data in the final published paper. (Lips-Wiersma and Hall, 2007: 779)

This quote nicely illustrates that quality is not just about conducting specific 'checks' but stems from careful consideration and execution of the whole research project.

We have already noted that Wyatt and Silvester's (2015) article on the career development of BME leaders is one of the few which discussed reflexivity as integral to their research. Involving a BME research colleague in the analysis was one decision they took as a result of reflexively considering issues of culture and ideology, with the aim of enabling their own assumptions as data analysts to be challenged, and ensuring they made their coding decisions explicit. Like Lips-Wiersma and Hall, they involved some of their original participants in a final quality check. However, where the latter simply asked for feedback on findings, Wyatt and Silvester asked managers to look at the actual coding relating to the template for their group (BME or white). They provide detail of one change in the organization of the templates as a result of this process. We feel that providing this kind of detail of quality procedures – plus inclusion of the two full templates – certainly adds to the persuasiveness of the article.

Our final example is Fernando and Cohen's (2011) study of the interplay between gender, organizational context and career in Sri Lanka. Unlike the previous two examples, this study did not use any kind of inter-coder comparison as a quality check. This is justifiable in an article that takes a social constructionist approach, in contrast to the realist stance in the previous papers. As Burr (1995) points out, social constructionism is wary of any attempt to privilege one version of reality over another. Instead the authors describe a very thorough collaborative approach to coding, that ensured critical reflection throughout and included an explicit search for deviant and minority voices within the accounts they analysed. The coherence between philosophical position and approach to ensuring quality of analysis is particularly commendable in this article.

We have given a good deal of space to the consideration of quality issues here because of their importance to advanced students engaged in research towards a Master's dissertation or similar. You must ensure that your overall research design and the way you carry it out enhances the quality of your analysis and the findings that stem from it. Demonstrating that the way you address quality is congruent with your philosophical and methodological position is crucial; for instance calculating inter-coder agreement made sense in Kidd's (2008) strongly realist study but examiners would take a dim view of a thesis using such a strategy while avowing a social constructionist stance. We would also emphasize the importance of being clear about how the actions you took in the name of quality actually impacted on your analysis. It is not enough simply to state that 'inter-coder comparison was used to challenge assumptions'; in a thesis you need to show what you did as a result of such challenges. Finally, we would urge you to take reflexivity seriously; demonstrate your awareness of how your own position and methodological choices may have shaped the research process and outcomes.

CHAPTER SUMMARY

This chapter has used the field of careers research as an exemplar of the different ways in which Template Analysis is used in qualitative business and management research. We have noted the range of philosophical positions taken by researchers, highlighting that more often than not this is not clearly and explicitly delineated in published articles. We have considered the types of data collection methods in evidence; unsurprisingly these are dominated by semi-structured interviews, but also include qualitative questionnaires and documentary analysis. We have seen that a *priori* themes are widely employed, varying in how they are derived and whether they can be considered as 'hard' or 'soft'. Finally, we have examined the ways in which quality issues are addressed by researchers in this area using Template Analysis.

Our exploration of this literature highlights some important points for students who wish to use Template Analysis in a Master's dissertation project.

- Your philosophical position needs to be explicitly stated and its implications worked through in all aspects of your design and analysis.
- Think about your choice of data collection methods – don't automatically chose conventional semi-structured interviews.
- A *priori* themes can be very useful for your analysis, though are not compulsory in Template Analysis. Think carefully about how you define and use them in relation to your methodology and its underpinning philosophy.

- It is very important to show how you have ensured the quality of your analysis, again relating this to your methodology and philosophy. Specific checks such as inter-coder comparisons can be very useful, but set these in a wider approach of care, rigour and critical thinking in all aspects of your research.
- Unless you are taking a strongly neo-positivist approach, incorporate – and demonstrate – reflexivity in your analysis.

6

STRENGTHS AND LIMITATIONS OF TEMPLATE ANALYSIS

INTRODUCTION

Now that you have learned what Template Analysis is, how it is carried out and how others have used it, the aim of this final chapter is to help you understand how best to use it for your project. To do this we will discuss in turn the *limitations and challenges* and the *strengths and opportunities* associated with this style of qualitative data analysis. We will conclude with a reminder of some of the key points made throughout the book about how to use Template Analysis as effectively as possible.

LIMITATIONS AND CHALLENGES

Any method of qualitative data analysis has limitations: aspects that are relatively under-developed, topic areas or data types with which it does not work well and so on. Equally, all methods create challenges for the researcher that can lead to poor analysis if they are not successfully met. As far as Template Analysis goes, some of these are common to many (perhaps all) types of thematic analysis while others are more specific to this style. We outline five main limitations and challenges below, with some suggestions as to how you may respond to them in your own work.

The generic nature of Template Analysis

As we saw right at the start of this book, Template Analysis is a generic form of data analysis – that is, it is not tied to a specific philosophical approach. This sets the challenge of working out your own philosophical (and sometime also theoretical) position and thinking through what this implies for the way you use the method. Given the often rather pragmatic and practical focus of much research in business and management, the main risk here is that you simply never think through and articulate your position. You will see plenty of examples in the literature where the philosophical stance of a study is barely touched on, as we noted in Chapter 5 in relation specifically to the careers literature. However, there is no such thing as a study that does not have a philosophical position; it is just that sometimes this is not made explicit. Without a clear, thought-through position, you may find it hard to justify the analytical decisions you have made and the conclusions you have drawn. There may also be incoherence between what you have done with your data and the claims you make in your interpretation. None of these things is likely to be looked upon with favour by an experienced academic assessing your work!

The points we have made above do not mean that we think all dissertations and theses from studies using Template Analysis need to include extensive and complex discussions of ontology and epistemology. Students vary in where their main interests lie with regard to their research projects; some enjoy and are comfortable with deep engagement with philosophical issues, while others are much more focused on what their findings tell them of relevance to real-world practice. The crucial thing, though, is that wherever you fall on that spectrum you present your philosophical position with clarity and employ it coherently throughout your work. Our two detailed fictionalized examples in Chapter 4 show how different philosophical and theoretical positions may be taken into account in how Template Analysis is used. Similarly, the studies from the careers literature reviewed in Chapter 5 illustrate how different analytical decisions follow on from the overall approach taken – for example, in how quality issues are addressed.

The fragmentation of accounts

One of the things that draws many researchers to qualitative approaches is the wish to understand experience from the perspective of the whole person in all their distinctiveness, rather than seeing them as an aggregation of variables. Template Analysis, like pretty much all thematic approaches, runs the risk of fragmenting accounts so that all we see are a set of themes that apply across a group of participants. This is more likely to happen the larger the sample used in a study. Your philosophical position will influence how important it is to maintain an holistic view of individual participants: it would be crucial to a phenomenological study, but much less of a concern in a large-scale evaluation taking a subtle realist approach. However, even in the latter kind of project we would argue that it is valuable to retain some holistic sense of the person. This may be achieved in analysis through strategies such as writing case summaries and in the presentation of findings through individual case studies (see Chapter 2 for more on these aspects of the method).

Procedure as prescription

From time to time we receive e-mails from students using Template Analysis that say something like this:

> I am using TA to look at change management and have interviewed 20 managers. My template has three top-level themes, eight second-level themes and 20 third-level themes. Is this right?

We hope that by now you can see that this is not a question to which we could provide a meaningful answer. Firstly, there is no one 'right' way to do Template Analysis, and secondly, the characteristics of a template depend on a whole set of aspects particular to the project in question: it's philosophical approach, the extent to which participants' experiences vary, the time and resource available for it, and so on. Nevertheless, it is fair to say that in writing about Template Analysis we have given considerable attention to the procedural steps that may be taken. For novice researchers (perhaps with a supervisor who does not have much qualitative research background) there can be an understandable temptation to follow procedures 'to the letter' as a way of allaying anxieties about an unfamiliar process. We have sought to address this in the current book and previous publications by providing examples of different ways in which the method can be used, and repeatedly emphasizing that we are offering suggestions rather than prescriptions. You can – and should – adapt any aspect of the method to suit the needs of your study, so long as you can justify your reasons for it, and show it to be consistent with your overall approach.

Too much flexibility

While the procedural presentation of Template Analysis can lead some people into difficulties through seeing it as rigidly prescriptive, others struggle with the flexibility of the method. This is especially so in relation to the freedom allowed in the nature of the coding structure. With the option to use integrative themes and other lateral connections between hierarchical clusters, plus the exhortation to code to as many levels as you need for the richest parts of the data, inexperienced data analysts can find themselves facing an unmanageably complex coding template.

If you find yourself drifting in this direction, there are a few points we would direct your attention to:

- Remember you haven't got to devise a specific theme for every point of potential interest in the data. Keep the most detailed coding to those areas which are both of evident importance to your participants and of clear relevance to your research question.
- Think about the purpose of your study and the time you have available; a final year undergraduate project would not be expected to produce as complex a template as we might see in a doctoral thesis.
- Bear in mind that the template is not only a way to help you to organize your thinking about your data; it is also contributes to your communication of that thinking to your readers.
- Following the previous point, remember that the template is an analytical tool – constructing a 'perfect' template is not the ultimate aim of your research!

Limited guidance on the final interpretation

While Template Analysis provides detailed procedures for coding and thematically organizing your data, it gives rather loose guidance on how you move from the point where you have coded all your data to the final interpretation of it. This is in contrast to some other approaches, both methodology-specific (e.g. Grounded Theory) and generic (e.g. Framework Analysis). There is a danger that this can lead to researchers simply summarizing what they have coded under each main theme, with little attempt to engage in more sophisticated interpretative thinking. We see this potential limitation as part and parcel of the flexibility and adaptability of Template Analysis, which are important strengths (as we discuss below). It would be very hard to come up with specific suggestions for developing the final interpretation that could apply both to a theory-driven study such as David's back pain and work participation project described in Chapter 4 *and* to Fernando and Cohen's (2011) social constructionist exploration of career and gender in Sri Lanka, as reviewed in Chapter 5. We have tried to address this challenge by giving a variety of examples of studies, both in this book and in other publications on Template Analysis (e.g. King, 2004, 2012; Brooks and King, 2014; Brooks et al., 2015).

STRENGTHS AND OPPORTUNITIES

Many of the strengths of Template Analysis and the opportunities for qualitative researchers that it affords are essentially the other side of the coin to the limitations and challenges discussed above. This underlines how important it is to think carefully about why and how you are using any method of data analysis; a technique that works very effectively in one context may be problematic in another.

Adaptability

A major strength of Template Analysis, as a style of thematic analysis, is its adaptability. We feel this is especially true for a field that is generally pragmatic in orientation like business and management research. The choices you make about whether and how to use *a priori* themes, when to develop the initial template, whether to use integrative themes or other lateral connections and so on enable you to tailor the technique to the needs of your particular project. This includes ensuring that your whole analysis is coherent with your philosophical and (where relevant) theoretical approach, and that it is sensitive to practical, real-world concerns of your project. This emphasis on adaptability raises the question of what is common or core to all forms of Template Analysis? Or, to put it another way, what features would one expect to be present if you want to call the analytic approach you have taken Template Analysis? While we have no interest in policing the boundaries of Template Analysis, we would highlight the following three features as being central to the technique:

1. *Development of an initial template*. We would be uncomfortable describing a thematic analysis as following the template style if it began by carrying out preliminary coding on the entire data set.
2. *Iterative development and application of the template*. The process of trying out the current version of the template on further data, modifying in the light of problems or limitations discovered, then reapplying (and so on) is at the heart of Template Analysis. A study which rushed from the initial to the final template with little attempt at iterative development could not constitute a proper use of this style of analysis.
3. *Flexibility in coding levels*. Template Analysis never uses a rigidly defined coding hierarchy, such that the number of coding levels and the type of code they represent are defined in advance. The type of themes defined and the number of levels should always be a function of what the analyst finds necessary to answer their research question in a particular study.

We do not consider the use of *a priori* themes to be a defining feature of Template Analysis; however, as we saw in Chapter 5, it is a very common feature. Anecdotal evidence suggests to us that the ability to incorporate *a priori* themes is commonly one of the reasons why researchers choose to use this style of analysis. So, it is fair to say that while *a priori* themes are not compulsory in Template Analysis, the permissibility of them is a core characteristic.

Balancing openness and structure

The flexibility of Template Analysis, especially in how the template is constructed, helps the technique to achieve a balance between openness and structure in coding. On the one hand, the relatively non-prescriptive approach to how the template should be organized encourages the researcher to retain an open-minded approach to the analysis. It is easy in the light of new data – or a reconsideration of previously coded data – to reconfigure hierarchical clusters of themes, to add (or remove) lateral links between them, and so on (as detailed in Chapter 2). On the other hand, the iterative process of developing an initial template, applying, modifying and reapplying, provides a systematic basis for analysis; if followed diligently you will not gloss over any tricky sections of data to interpret or retain ill-defined themes.

Efficiency

It may seem strange to cite efficiency as a virtue in a qualitative data analysis method, given the emphasis in qualitative research on exploring data in depth and developing nuanced interpretations. We entirely agree that qualitative analysis should be carried out in as thorough a way as possible, but all projects have limits in terms of the time and other resources available for them. When you are facing the deadline for your dissertation or thesis, these limits are very real! We have found across numerous projects we have carried out ourselves, or supervised, that the front-loading of analytical work in Template Analysis usually results in a more efficient use of time across the analysis as a whole. What we mean by this is that when you work in a very thorough and detailed way to develop your initial template, subsequent coding and development of the template towards its final version usually goes quite smoothly. In addition, the flexibility we have highlighted means that you can make choices about the depth of analysis in line with the time and resource available to you. In an undergraduate project you might decide to identify one or two main themes as highly relevant to your research question and only develop these to multiple levels of coding. In contrast, in a PhD the template may be much more elaborated as a whole.

One consequence of the efficiency of Template Analysis is that it tends to enable you to analyse more cases than you would with other methods. For example, in a 12-month Master's by research project culminating in an 25,000 word dissertation, we might recommend that a student using a method such as IPA (Smith et al., 2009) carries out no more than eight to ten in-depth interviews in total. If using Template Analysis they could manage up to twice that number. This is not to say that a larger sample is always a good thing in itself in qualitative research, but having the capacity to include more participants may provide worthwhile opportunities for your research design. For instance, it may enable you to sample across a wider range of occupational groups within an organization.

Transparency

The focus in Template Analysis on the development of the coding template itself means that so long as a good record is kept of how and why successive versions change, there is a high degree of transparency to the analytical process. This has advantages for the auditability of your analysis – the extent to which you can trace and account for the way your coding and interpretation developed – which can be a significant aspect of quality assurance in qualitative analysis (Carcary, 2009). Equally, a good record of how your coding – and the thinking behind it – evolved may be very helpful in facilitating methodological reflexivity (Finlay, 2003). This refers to a researcher's ability to reflect on the methodological choices they made and consider how they have shaped the direction of the analysis. Remember that showing you have paid attention to the quality of your analysis and have taken a suitably reflexive approach to it are hallmarks of a well-conducted qualitative project. Finally, if you used any kind of independent coding as part of your analytical quality assurance strategy, a thorough audit trail can help you to highlight how such a process led to specific developments in your template.

CONCLUSION: GETTING THE BEST FROM TEMPLATE ANALYSIS

In this book we have taken you through an account of what Template Analysis is and how to use it taking into account the philosophical issues that should shape your analytical choices. We have provided examples of the kind of projects you might carry out at Master's level, and examined the use of the technique in published literature in business and management research. We trust you now feel well prepared to embark on your own qualitative research, using this style of analysis. As a final aid to your engagement with Template Analysis, we have provided in Table 6.1 a summary of key advice relating to each main stage of the data analysis process – and your preparation for it – with references back to earlier chapters.

Table 6.1   A reminder of key advice for the successful use of Template Analysis

BEFORE YOUR STUDY STARTS	
Your philosophical position	What is your ontological and epistemological position? What does this imply for how you should use Template Analysis? (See Chapter 2.)
Your theoretical position	Are you drawing on a particular theory or theoretical approach? If so, is it consistent with your philosophical position? Consider whether it makes sense to capture some key concepts from your theoretical position through the use of *a priori* themes. (See especially Chapter 3.)

(Continued)

Table 6.1   (Continued)

BEFORE YOUR STUDY STARTS	
Your methodological position	Are your research question(s) and all aspects of your research design (e.g. sampling, data collection methods, quality assurance approach) coherent with each other and with your philosophical/theoretical position(s)? Regarding use of Template Analysis, the most likely areas where you may find misalignment with overall methodology are: • failure to properly address research question(s) • defining themes in a manner that conflicts with your approach • using inappropriate quality procedures. (See below, and discussions of methodological coherence in Chapters 3, 4 and 5.)

AT THE START OF ANALYSIS	
Confirm/decide on *a priori* themes	By definition, *a priori* themes must be defined before analysis starts. Decide now whether you want to include any, and define them now. (See Chapter 3, and discussions of use of *a priori* themes in Chapters 4 and 5.)
The mechanics of analysis: using CAQDAS	Are you going to use specialist software (i.e. CAQDAS programs such as NVivo, MaxQDA and Atlas.ti) for your analysis? From the start, or only after the initial template stage? Make sure you are competent with the software before starting! (See Chapter 3.)
The mechanics of analysis: using general software	You may want to use general software such as Word, Excel or equivalents to help with your analysis. Again, make sure you know how to use them for the purposes of analysis. (See Chapter 3.)
The mechanics of analysis: by hand	If you are doing all your analysis by hand, or even just the first stages, you need to be well organized about your procedures and practices. In particular, make sure you keep an accurate record of the development of your template. (See Chapter 3, and the second example in Chapter 4.)

DURING ANALYSIS	
Constructing the Initial Template	Think carefully about how soon to construct the initial template. Remember the rule of thumb that the more diverse your data set, the more data items (such as transcripts, or observation session notes) you'll need to include before you're ready for this stage. (See Chapters 3 and 4.)
Developing the template – getting unstuck	As you iteratively develop later versions of the template you may find that you get 'stuck' in certain areas – themes just don't seem to 'work' to cover some sections of the data, despite repeated attempts to re-define them. If this happens, try something more radical; for example, could you turn a

	cluster on its head, so that what was a low-level theme becomes high level (and vice versa)? Involving an independent coder at such a point can also help. (See Chapters 3 and 4.)
Deciding on the 'final' version of the template	The template will never be perfect; at some point – as your submission deadline approaches - you have to decide its 'good enough' and stop! You want to be sure that every section of your data relevant to your research question(s) is coded to your template, and that the template itself is as clear and coherent as possible, without sacrificing inclusivity. (See Chapters 3 and 4.)
Ensuring and demonstrating quality in analysis	You should have a good idea of your proposed quality assurance strategy before you start your analysis, but you may need to supplement or adapt them in the light of how the analysis proceeds (see the comment above about 'getting unstuck' in template development). Make sure you use practices and procedures that are in line with your philosophical and methodological approach. (See Chapters 3 and 5.)

WRITING UP

Presentation of findings	Consider what the best way to present your findings will be, making use of the potential of the template to structure this. Do you organize around main themes, highlight key themes within a case-by-case approach, or a mixture of the two? (See Chapter 3.)
Presentation of template	Think about how best to present your template(s) in your thesis. You should consider whether to include the full version of your final template, or a reduced version with the full one in an appendix. You should also consider whether to use the conventional 'linear' form or a 'mind map' style – or indeed come up with a creative solution of your own! (See Chapter 3.)
Use of appendices	You can use your appendices to show different stages of the development of your thesis, and perhaps annotated extracts of data illustrating how themes have been used. (See Chapter 3.)

Important though it is to read about any method before employing it, and to keep engaged with the relevant methodological literature, in the end there is no substitute for actually doing it. We still learn something new about how to use Template Analysis effectively with every study in which we use it. We wish you all the best in your own encounters with qualitative research in business and management, and hope you find that Template Analysis serves you well.

REFERENCES

Alarcon, P., Wieland, B., Mateus, A. and Dewberry, C. (2014) Pig farmers' perceptions, attitudes, influences and management of information in the decision-making process for disease control. *Preventive Veterinary Medicine*, 116 (3): 223–242.

Archer, M., Bhaskar, R., Collier, A., Lawson, T. and Norrie, A. (eds) (1998) *Critical Realism: Essential Readings*. London: Routledge.

Arribas-Ayllon, M. and Walkerdine, V. (2008) Foucauldian discourse analysis. In C. Willig and W. Stainton-Rogers (eds), *The SAGE Handbook of Qualitative Research in Psychology*. London: SAGE, pp. 91–108.

Bakker, A.B. and Demerouti, E. (2007) The job demands-resources model: state of the art. *Journal of Managerial Psychology*, 22 (3): 309–328.

Bell, E. and Thorpe, R. (2013) *A Very Short, Fairly Interesting and Reasonably Cheap Book About Management Research*. London: SAGE.

Blumberg, B.F., Cooper, D.R. and Schindler, P.S. (2014) *Business Research Methods* (4th edn). Maidenhead: McGraw-Hill.

Brannan, M.J. and Oultram, T. (2012) Participant observation. In G. Symon and C. Cassell (eds), *Qualitative Organizational Research: Core Methods and Current Challenges*. London: SAGE, pp. 296–313.

Braun, V. and Clarke, V. (2006) Using thematic analysis in psychology. *Qualitative Research in Psychology*, 3 (2): 77–101.

Braun, V. and Clarke, V. (2013) *Successful Qualitative Research: A Practical Guide for Beginners*. London: SAGE.

Brooks, J. and King, N. (2014) Doing template analysis: evaluating an end-of-life care service. *SAGE Research Methods Cases*. doi: 10.4135/978144627305013512755.

Brooks, J., King, N. and Wearden, A. (2014) Couples' experiences of interacting with outside others in chronic fatigue syndrome: a qualitative study. *Chronic Illness*, 10 (1): 5–17.

Brooks, J.M., McCluskey, S., King, N. and Burton, A.K. (2013) Illness perceptions in the context of differing work participation outcomes: exploring the influence of significant others in persistent back pain. *BMC Musculoskeletal Disorders*, 14: 48. doi:10.1186/1471-2474-14-48.

Brooks, J., McCluskey, S., Turley, E. and King, N. (2015) The utility of template analysis in qualitative psychology research. *Qualitative Research in Psychology*, 12 (2): 202–222.

Brooks, R. and Youngson, P.L. (2014) Undergraduate work placements: an analysis of the effects on careers progression. *Studies in Higher Education*, 41 (9): 1563-1578

Bryman, A. and Bell, E. (2015) *Business Research Methods* (4th edn). Oxford: Oxford University Press.

Burr, V. (1995) *An Introduction to Social Constructionism*. London: Routledge.

Butt, T. and Burr, V. (2004) *Invitation to Personal Construct Psychology* (2nd edn). London: Whurr.

Carcary, M. (2009) The research audit trial: enhancing trustworthiness in qualitative inquiry. *The Electronic Journal of Business Research Methods*, 7 (1): 11-24.

Cassell, C., Buehring, A., Symon, G. and Johnson, P. (2005) *Benchmarking Good Practice in Qualitative Management Research*. Swindon: ESRC Research Report.

Charmaz, K. (2014) *Constructing Grounded Theory* (2nd edn). London: SAGE.

Clarke, C.A. and Knights, D. (2015) Careering through academia: securing identities or engaging ethical subjectivities? *Human Relations*, 68 (12): 1865-1888.

Cohen, L., Duberley, J. and Mallon, M. (2004) Social constructionism in the study of career: accessing the parts that other approaches cannot reach. *Journal of Vocational Behavior*, 64 (3): 407-422.

Corbin, J. and Strauss, A. (2015) *Basics of Qualitative Research: Techniques and Procedures for Developing Grounded Theory* (4th edn). Thousand Oaks, CA: SAGE.

Corsaro, D. and Snehota, I. (2011) Alignment and misalignment in business relationships. *Industrial Marketing Management*, 40 (6): 1042-1054.

Crabtree, B.F. and Miller, W.L. (1992) A template approach to text analysis: developing and using codebooks. In B.F. Crabtree and W.L. Miller (eds), *Doing Qualitative Research*. Newbury Park, CA: SAGE, pp. 93-109.

Creswell, J. (2007) *Qualitative Inquiry and Research Design* (2nd edn). Thousand Oaks, CA: SAGE.

Denzin, N.K. and Lincoln, Y.S. (2005) Introduction: the discipline and practice of qualitative research. In N.K. Denzin and Y.S. Lincoln (eds), *The SAGE Handbook of Qualitative Research* (3rd edn). Thousand Oaks, CA: SAGE, pp. 1-42.

Dey, I. (1993) *Qualitative Data Analysis: A User-Friendly Guide for Social Scientists*. Abingdon: Routledge.

Dickmann, M. and Cerdin, J.L. (2014) Boundaryless career drivers: exploring macro-contextual factors in location decisions. *Journal of Global Mobility*, 2 (1): 26-52.

Dries, N. and Pepermans, R. (2008) 'Real' high potential careers: an empirical study into the perspectives of organisations and high potentials. *Personnel Review*, 37 (1): 85-108.

Duberley, J., Johnson, P. and Cassell, C. (2012) Philosophies underpinning qualitative research. In G. Symon and C. Cassell (eds), *Qualitative Organizational Research: Core Methods and Current Challenges*. London: SAGE, pp. 15-34.

Fernando, W.D.A. and Cohen, L. (2011) Exploring the interplay between gender, organizational context and career: a Sri Lankan perspective. *Career Development International*, 16 (6): 553-571.

Figueiras, M.J. and Weinman, J. (2003) Do similar patient and spouse perceptions of myocardial infarction predict recovery? *Psychology and Health*, 18 (2): 201-216.

Finlay, L. (2003) The reflexive journey: mapping multiple routes. In L. Finlay and B. Gough (eds), *Reflexivity: A Practical Guide for Researchers in Health and Social Sciences*. Oxford: Blackwell, pp. 3-20.

Finlay, L. (2009) Debating phenomenological research methods. *Phenomenology & Practice*, 3 (1): 6-25.

Frambach, J., Driessen, E., Beh, P. and Van der Vleuten, C. (2014) Quiet or questioning? Students' discussion behaviors in student-centered education across cultures. *Studies in Higher Education*, 39 (6): 1001–1021.

Frost, N., Nolas, S.M., Brooks-Gordon, B., Esin, C., Holt, A., Mehdizadeh, L. and Shinebourne, P. (2010) Pluralism in qualitative research: the impact of different researchers and qualitative approaches on the analysis of qualitative data. *Qualitative Research*, 10 (4): 441–460.

Gee, J.P. (2014) *An Introduction to Discourse Analysis: Theory and Method* (4th edn). Abingdon: Routledge.

Geertz, C. (1973) *The Interpretation of Cultures*. New York: Basic Books.

Gibbs, G. (2002) *Qualitative Data Analysis: Explorations with NVivo*. Buckingham: Open University.

Giorgi, A. and Giorgi, B. (2008) Phenomenology. In J. Smith (ed.), *Qualitative Psychology: A Practical Guide to Research Methods* (2nd edn). London: SAGE, pp. 26–52.

Glaser, B. and Strauss, A. (1967) *The Discovery of Grounded Theory: Strategies for Qualitative Research*. Mill Valley, CA: Sociology Press.

Hahn, C. (2008) *Doing Qualitative Research Using Your Computer: A Practical Guide*. London: SAGE.

Hammersley, M. (1992) Ethnography and realism. In M. Hammersley (ed.), *What's Wrong with Ethnography? Methodological Explorations*. London: Routledge, pp. 43–56.

Hayes, N. (1997) Theory-led thematic analysis: social identification in small companies. In N. Hayes (ed.), *Doing Qualitative Analysis in Psychology*. Hove, UK: Psychology Press, pp. 93–114.

Haynes, K. (2012) Reflexivity in qualitative research. In G. Symon and C. Cassell (eds), *Qualitative Organizational Research: Core Methods and Current Challenges*. London: SAGE, pp. 72–89.

Hsieh, H.-F. and Shannon, S. (2005) Three approaches to qualitative content analysis. *Qualitative Health Research*, 15 (9): 1277–1288.

Hughes, B., Wareham, J. and Joshi, I. (2010) Doctors' online information needs, cognitive search strategies, and judgments of information quality and cognitive authority: how predictive judgments introduce bias into cognitive search models. *Journal of the American Society for Information Science and Technology*, 61 (3): 433–452.

Jefferson, G. (1984) Transcription notation. In J. Atkinson and J. Heritage (eds), *Structures of Social Interaction: Studies in Conversation Analysis*. New York: Cambridge University Press, pp. 346–369.

Johnson, P. (2004) Analytic Induction. In C. Cassell and G. Symon (eds), *Essential Guide to Qualitative Methods in Organizational Research*. London: SAGE, pp. 165–179.

Johnson, P., Buehring, A., Cassell, C. and Symon, G. (2006) Evaluating qualitative management research: towards a contingent criteriology. *International Journal of Management Reviews*, 8 (3): 131–156.

Kandola, B. (2012) Focus groups. In G. Symon and C. Cassell (eds), *Qualitative Organizational Research: Core Methods and Current Challenges*. London: SAGE, pp. 258–274.

Kelliher, C. and Anderson, D. (2010) Doing more with less? Flexible working practices and the intensification of work. *Human Relations*, 63 (1): 83–106.

Khokher, S.Y. and Beauregard, T.A. (2014) Work-family attitudes and behaviours among newly immigrant Pakistani expatriates: the role of organizational family-friendly policies. *Community, Work & Family*, 17 (2): 142–162.

Kidd, J. M. (2008) Exploring the components of career well-being and the emotions associated with significant career experiences. *Journal of Career Development*, 35 (2): 166–186.

Kiffin-Petersen, S., Murphy, S. and Soutar, F. (2012) The problem-solving service worker: appraisal mechanisms and positive affective experiences during customer interactions. *Human Relations*, 65 (9): 1179–1206.

King, N. (1998) Template analysis. In G. Symon and C. Cassell (eds), *Qualitative Methods and Analysis in Organizational Research: A Practical Guide*. London: SAGE, pp. 118–134.

King, N. (2004) Using templates in the qualitative analysis of text. In C. Cassell and G. Symon (eds), *Essential Guide to Qualitative Methods in Organizational Research*. London: SAGE, pp. 256–270.

King, N. (2012) Doing template analysis. In G. Symon and C. Cassell (eds), *Qualitative Organizational Research: Core Methods and Current Challenges*. London: SAGE, pp. 426–450.

King, N., Bailey, J. and Newton, P. (1994) Analysing general practitioners' referral decisions: I. Developing an analytical framework. *Family Practice*, 11: 3–8.

King, N., Bravington, A., Brooks, J., Hardy, B., Melvin, J. and Wilde, D. (2013) The Pictor Technique: a method for exploring the experience of collaborative working. *Qualitative Health Research*, 23 (8): 1138–1152.

King, N. and Horrocks, C. (2010) *Interviews in Qualitative Research*. London: SAGE.

King, N., Melvin, J., Ashby, J. and Firth, J. (2010) Community palliative care: role perception. *British Journal of Community Nursing*, 15 (2): 91–98.

King, N., Roche, T. and Frost C.D. (2000) Diverse identities, common purpose: multi-disciplinary clinical supervision in primary care. *Proceedings of the British Psychological Society Occupational Psychology Conference*, Brighton, 5–7 January, pp. 199–204.

Kracauer, S. (1952) The challenge of qualitative content analysis. *The Public Opinion Quarterly*, 16 (4): 631–642.

Langdridge, D. (2007) *Phenomenological Psychology: Theory, Research and Method*. Harlow: Pearson.

Lee, B. (2012) Using documents in organizational research. In G. Symon and C. Cassell (eds), *Qualitative Organizational Research: Core Methods and Current Challenges*. London: SAGE, pp. 389–407.

Lincoln, Y.S. (1995) Emerging criteria for quality in qualitative and interpretive research. *Qualitative Inquiry*, 1: 275–289.

Lincoln, Y.S. and Guba, E.G. (1985) *Naturalistic Inquiry*. Newbury Park, CA: SAGE.

Lips-Wiersma, M. and Hall, D.T. (2007) Organizational career development is not dead: a case study on managing the new career during organizational change. *Journal of Organizational Behavior*, 28 (6): 771–792.

Madill, A., Jordan, A. and Shirley, C. (2000) Objectivity and reliability in qualitative analysis: realist, contextualist and radical constructionist epistemologies. *British Journal of Psychology*, 91 (1): 1–20.

Maguire, J.S. (2008) Leisure and the obligation of self-work: an examination of the fitness field. *Leisure Studies*, 27 (1): 59–75.

Mallon, M. and Cohen, L. (2001) Time for a change? Women's accounts of the move from organizational careers to self-employment. *British Journal of Management*, 12 (3): 217–230.

Maniadakis, N. and Gray, A. (2000) The economic burden of back pain the UK. *Pain*, 84 (1): 95–103.

Maxwell, J.A. (2012) *A Realist Approach for Qualitative Research*. London: SAGE.

Maznevski, M. and Chudoba, K. (2000) Bridging space over time: global virtual team dynamics and effectiveness. *Organization Studies*, 11 (5): 473–492.

McAdams, D.P. (1993) *The Stories We Live By: Personal Myths and the Making of the Self*. London: Guilford Press.

McCluskey, S., Brooks, J.M., King, N. and Burton, A.K. (2011) The influence of 'significant others' on persistent back pain and work participation: a qualitative exploration of illness perceptions. *BMC Musculoskeletal Disorders*, 12: 236. doi:10.1186/1471-2474-12-236.

Miles, M. and Huberman, A. (1994) *Qualitative Data Analysis: An Expanded Sourcebook* (2nd edn). Thousand Oaks, CA: SAGE.

Morgan, A. and Ziglio, E. (2007) Revitalising the evidence base for public health: an assets model. *IUHPE – Promotion & Education*, Supplement (2): 17-22.

Moss-Morris, R., Weinman, J., Petrie, K.J., Horne, R., Cameron, L.D. and Buick, D. (2002) The revised Illness Perception Questionnaire (IPQ-R). *Psychology and Health*, 17 (1): 1-16.

Moustakas, C. (1994) *Phenomenological Research Methods*. London: SAGE.

Myers, M.D. (2013) *Qualitative Research in Business and Management* (2nd edn). London: SAGE.

Nadin, S. and Cassell, C. (2004) Using data matrices. In C. Cassell and G. Symon (eds), *Essential Guide to Qualitative Methods in Organizational Research*. London: SAGE, pp. 271-287.

NICE (National Institute for Health and Care Excellence) (2014) Community engagement to improve health. *NICE Local Government Briefings*. Available from http://publications.nice.org.uk/lgb16 (accessed 24 June 2016).

Palmer, K.T., Walsh, K., Bendall, H., Cooper, C. and Coggon, D. (2000) Back pain in Britain: comparison of two prevalence surveys at an interval of 10 years. *British Medical Journal*, 320 (7249): 1577-1578.

Pattinson, S. and Preece, D. (2014) Communities of practice, knowledge acquisition and innovation: a case-study of science-based SMEs. *Journal of Knowledge Management*, 18 (1): 107.

Phillips, C., Main, C., Buck, R., Aylward, M., Wynne-Jones, G. and Farr, A. (2008) Prioritising pain in policy making: the need for a whole systems perspective. *Health Policy*, 88 (2-3): 166-175.

Point, S. and Dickmann, M. (2012) Branding international careers: an analysis of multinational corporations' official wording. *European Management Journal*, 30 (1): 18-31.

Poland, B.D. (2002) Transcription quality. In J.F. Gubrium and J.A. Holstein (eds), *Handbook of Interview Research: Context & Method*. Thousand Oaks, CA: SAGE, pp. 629-650.

Poppleton, S., Briner, R. and Kiefer, T. (2008) The roles of context and everyday experience in understanding work-non-work relationships: a qualitative diary study of white- and blue-collar workers. *Journal of Occupational and Organizational Psychology*, 81 (3): 481-502.

Potter, J. (2012) Discourse analysis and discursive psychology. In H. Cooper (editor-in-chief). *APA Handbook of Research Methods in Psychology: Vol. 2. Quantitative, Qualitative, Neuropsychological, and Biological*. Washington: American Psychological Association Press, pp. 111-130.

Pritchard, K. (2012) Combing qualitative methods. In G. Symon and C. Cassell (eds), *Qualitative Organizational Research: Core Methods and Current Challenges*. London: SAGE, pp. 132-148.

Public Health England (2015) *Health and Wellbeing: A Guide to Community-Centred Approaches*. Available from www.gov.uk/government/publications/health-and-wellbeing-a-guide-to-community-centred-approaches (accessed 24 June 2016).

Putnam, H. (1999) *The Threefold Cord: Mind, Body and World*. New York: Columbia University Press.

Radcliffe, L.S. (2013) Qualitative diaries: uncovering the complexities of work-life decision-making. *Qualitative Research in Organizations and Management*, 8 (2): 163-180.

Reicher, S. (2000) Against methodolatry: some comments on Elliott, Fischer and Rennie. *British Journal of Clinical Psychology*, 39 (1): 1-6.

Ritchie, J. and Spencer, L. (1994) Qualitative data analysis for applied policy research. In A. Bryman and R.G. Burgess (eds), *Analyzing Qualitative Data*. London: Routledge, pp. 173-194.

Saldaña, J. (2009) *The Coding Manual for Qualitative Researchers*. Thousand Oaks, CA: SAGE.

Shaw, C. and Wainwright, D. (2007) Developing a CSF causal loop model for managing IT projects: a case study of an inter-organisational healthcare pathology IT system. *Proceedings of 28th International Conference on Information Systems*, Montreal.

Smith, J.A., Flowers, P. and Larkin, M. (2009) *Interpretative Phenomenological Analysis: Theory, Method and Research*. London: SAGE.

Spencer, L., Ritchie, J., Lewis, J. and Dillon, L. (2003) *Quality in Qualitative Evaluation: A Framework for Assessing Research Evidence*. Report from the Cabinet Office, UK.

Spitzer, W.O., LeBlanc, F.E., Dupuis, M. et al. (1987) Scientific approach to the assessment and management of activity-related spinal disorders: a monograph for clinicians. Report of the Quebec Task Force on Spinal Disorders. *Spine*, 12 (7): S1–S59.

Symon, G. and Cassell, C. (2012) Assessing qualitative research. In G. Symon and C. Cassell (eds), *Qualitative Organizational Research: Core Methods and Current Challenges*. London: SAGE, pp. 205–223.

Taylor, G.W. and Ussher, J.M. (2001). Making sense of S&M: a discourse analytic account. *Sexualities*, 4, 293–314.

Tomkins, L. and Eatough, V. (2010) Reflecting on the use of IPA with focus groups: pitfalls and potentials. *Qualitative Research in Psychology*, 7 (3): 244–262.

Tomkins, L. and Eatough, V. (2014) Stop 'helping' me! Identity, recognition and agency in the nexus of work and care. *Organization*, 21 (1): 3–21.

Tracy, S. (2010) Qualitative quality: eight 'big tent' criteria for excellent qualitative research. *Qualitative Inquiry*, 16 (10): 837–851.

Vaag, J., Giæver, F. and Bjerkeset, O. (2014) Specific demands and resources in the career of the Norwegian freelance musician. *Arts & Health: An International Journal for Research, Policy and Practice*, 6 (3): 205–222.

Van Assen, M., Van den Berg, G. and Pietersma, P. (2008) *Key Management Models: The 60+ Models Every Manager Needs to Know*. London: FT Prentice Hall.

Van Tulder, M. and Koes, B. (2002) Low back pain and sciatica (chronic). *Clinical Evidence*, 7: 1032–1048.

Waddell, G. and Burton, K. (2006) *Is Work Good for Your Health?* London: The Stationery Office.

Waddell, G., Burton, K. and Kendall, N. (2008) *Vocational Rehabilitation: What Works, for Whom, and When?* London: The Stationery Office.

Waddington, K. (2005) Using diaries to explore the characteristics of work-related gossip: methodological considerations from exploratory multimethod research. *Journal of Occupational and Organizational Psychology*, 78 (2): 221–236.

Wang, X.L. and Bowie, D. (2009) Revenue management: the impact on business-to-business relationships. *Journal of Services Marketing*, 23 (1): 31–41.

Wetherell, M., Taylor, S. and Yates, S.J. (2001) *Discourse as Data: A Guide for Analysis*. London: SAGE.

Whiting, L., Kendall, S. and Wills, W. (2012) An asset-based approach: an alternative health promotion strategy? *Community Practitioner*, 85 (1): 25–28.

Wyatt, M. and Silvester, J. (2015) Reflections on the labyrinth: investigating black and minority ethnic leaders' career experiences. *Human Relations*, 68 (8): 1243–1269.

Yardley, L. (2008) Demonstrating validity in qualitative psychology. In J. Smith (ed.), *Qualitative Psychology: A Practical Guide to Research Methods* (2nd edn). London: SAGE, pp. 235–251.

Zikic, J. and Richardson, J. (2007) Unlocking the careers of business professionals following job loss: sensemaking and career exploration of older workers. *Canadian Journal of Administrative Sciences*, 24 (1): 58–73.

INDEX

Note: Page numbers in *italic type* refer to figures and tables.

a priori themes, 3, 11, 29-30, 89, *92*
  in case examples, 49-50, 58, 60-1, 71, *76-7*, 80
  and philosophical position of
    research, 18, 19, 20
adaptability, 89
  see also flexibility
analytic induction, 6
appendices, 43, *93*
application of templates, 4, 35-7, 53-4,
  60, 65-7, 89
asset approach (case example), 58-71
asynchronous online interviews, 8
audience appeal, 23
audit trail, 21, 25, 36, *41*, 91

back pain (case example), 48-58
Brooks, J., 3, 35
business and management research
  template analysis in context of, 7-12
  see also careers literature examples

CAQDAS, 27, 30, 31, 49, 53, *92*
career drivers (case example), 74, *76*, 79, 80
careers literature examples, 73-7
  a priori themes, *76-7*, 80
  methods, *76-7*, 79
  philosophical position, *76-7*, 78-9
  quality of analysis, *76-7*, 81-3
case examples of template analysis, 47
  careers literature examples, 73-83
  HR example, 48-58
  public health example, 58-71
case studies, in presentation of work, 42, 67
case summaries, advantages of, 31-3, 38, 42
Cassell, C., 40

Cerdin, J.L., 74, *76*, *79*, 80
clustering, 3, 33-4, 53, 61
codes, relationship with themes, 28-9
coding
  of asynchronous online interviews, 8
  independent *see* independent coding
  preliminary, 3, 27-33, 49-51, 60-1
coding by hand, 27-8, 60, *92*
coding levels, 3, 34-5, 89
coding structure (template), 6-7, 25-6
Cohen, L., 74, 75, 76, 77, 78, 80, 82
community engagement (case example), 58-71
confirmability, 82
constructionist approach
  and quality, 81, 82
  radical constructionism, 21-3, 39-40
constructivist epistemology, 18, 19, 60
contextualist approach, 19-21, 39-40
Crabtree, B.F., 2
credibility, 82
critical realism, 15, 18, 19
cross-sectional design, 10

data
  familiarization with, 3, 27, 49, 60
  interpretation of, 4, 37-8, 57, 67, 88
  types for temporal analysis, 7-10
deductive reasoning, 6
dependability, 82
depth of coding, 35, 89
descriptive coding, 7, 26
development of templates, 35-7, 53-4, 65-7,
  89, *92-3*
diagrammatic presentation of template, 43, *45*
diary methods, 8-9

Dickmann, M., 74, *76*, 79, 80
documentary analysis, 79
documentary data, 10
    see also written accounts
Duberley, J., 16

e-mail interviews, 8
Eatough, V., 8
ecological validity, 39
efficiency, 90
epistemology, 14, 16, 78
    of contextualism, 19
    of limited realism, 18
    of qualitative neo-positivism, 17
    of radical constructionism, 22

falsification, 15
familiarization with data, 3, 27, 49, 60
feedback, *41*, 67, 81, 82
Fernando, W.D.A., 74, *76*, 78, 80, 82
final interpretation, 4, 37-8, 57, 67, 88
final template, 4, 54-7, 67-71, *93*
flexibility, 25-6, 87-8, 89
focus groups, 8, 60
fragmentation of accounts, 86-7

gender and career (case example), 74, 76, 80, 82
generic methodology, 5-6, 86
grounded theory, 5, 6
group interviews, 8, 60
Guba, E.G., 82

Hahn, C., 31
Hall, D.T., 74-5, 77, 80, 81-2
hand (analysis by), 27-8, 60, *92*
hierarchical coding, 3, 34-5, 89
holistic view, 86-7
Horrocks, C., 15, 28
hypothetico-deductivism, 15

Illness Perception Questionnaire (IPQ), 49
independent coding, *41*, 91
    in case examples, 52, 61, 81
    and philosophical position, 17-18, 19, 21
inductive reasoning, 6
initial templates, 3, 34-5, 51-2, 61-5, 89, *92*
integrative themes, 35, 54
inter-group comparisons, 10-11
inter-rater reliability, 18
internal coherence, 23
interpretation of data, 4, 37-8, 57, 67, 88
interpretative phenomenological analysis
    (IPA), 5, 6
interpretive coding, 7, 26
interpretivism, 14

interview data, 7-8
interviews
    case examples of, 49, 60
    in case summaries, 32-3
    popularity of, 79
    types of, 8

Kidd, J.M., 9, 74, *76*, 79, 81
King, N., 2-3, 15, 28, 35
Kracauer, S., 2

language, 22
limitations, of template analysis, 85-8
limited realism, 18-19, 59-60
Lincoln, Y.S., 82
line-numbering, 27-8, 33-4
linear presentation of template, 43-4
Lips-Wiersma, M., 74-5, 77, 80, 81-2
longitudinal studies, 11

Madill, A., 16, 23
Mallon, M., 75, 77, 78
Maxwell, J.A., 19
methodological reflexivity, 21, 91
methodology
    considering, *92*
    definition, 14
    link with method, 2, 5-6, 16
    and philosophical position, 5-6, 86
    specific vs generic approaches, 5-6
methods
    careers literature examples, *76-7*, 79
    definition, 13-14
    link with methodology, 2, 5-6, 16
    mixed methods studies, 11, 17, 38, 79
    see also interviews
Miller, W.L., 2
mind maps, 43, *45*
mixed methods studies, 11, 17, 38, 79
modifications *see* development of templates

narrative analysis, 38
natural realism, 18
neo-positivism *see* qualitative neo-positivism
NVivo, 30

observational studies, 9
online interviews, 8
Online QDA site, 30
ontology, 14, 15, 16
    of contextualism, 19
    of limited realism, 18
    of qualitative neo-positivism, 17
    of radical constructionism, 22
openness, of template organisation, 89-90

organizational change (case example), 74-5,
77, 80, 81-2
organizational documents, 10

parallel coding, 35
participant diaries, 8-9
participant quotes, *41, 42*
participants, feedback from, *41*, 81, 82
patterns of themes, 37
phenomenology, 20
philosophical position
in case examples, 48-9, 59-60, *76-7*, 78-9
considering, *91*
contextualist, 19-21
distinguishing, 16-23
implications for template analysis, 16, 17-19,
20-1, 22-3
importance of, 78-9, 86
limited realist, 18-19
and methodology, 5-6, 86
qualitative neo-positivism, 16-18
and quality criteria, 18, 19, 22-3, 39-40, 81,
82, 83
radical constructionist, 21-3
understanding, 13-15
Pictor visual method, 32
placeholder codes, 28-9
Point, S., 79
positivism, 14-15
qualitative neo-positivism, 16-18, 39, 48-9, 81
post-positivism, 15
preliminary coding, 3, 27-33, 49-51, 60-1
presentation of findings, 67, *93*
presentation of template, 42-5, *93*
public health project (case example), 58-71

qualitative data analysis
quality checks, 40-1
template analysis in context of, 4
qualitative evaluation studies, 11
qualitative neo-positivism, 16-18, 39, 48-9, 81
qualitative pluralism, 38
qualitative questionnaires, 9, 79
qualitative research
epistemology and ontology in, 14
quality criteria in, 39-40
quality of analysis, 91, *93*
quality checks, 40-1
case examples, 52, 61, 67, *76-7*, 81-3
quality criteria, 39-40
and philosophical position, 18, 19, 22-3,
39-40, 81, 82, 83
quantitative research, 14-15, 39
questionnaires (qualitative), 9, 79
quotations, *41, 42*

race and ethnicity (case example), 75, 77, 79,
80, 81, 82
radical constructionism, 21-3, 39-40
realist approach, 15, 16-17, 39, 78, 81
critical realism, 15, 18, 19
limited realism, 18-19, 59-60
records *see* audit trail
reflexivity
approaches to, 18, 19, 20-1, 23
and audit trail, *41*
case examples, 67, 81, 82
importance of, 83, 91
Reicher, S., 16
relativist approach, 15, 22
reliability, 18, 39
research journals, 21
research settings and topics, 11-12
respondents *see* participants

Saldaña, J., 5
sample size, 90
self-employment (case example), 75, 77, 78
semi-structured interviews, 8
Silvester, J., 75, 77, 79, 80, 81, 82
social constructionism *see* constructionist
approach
software
CAQDAS, 27, 30, 31, 49, 53, *92*
general word processing, 27-8, 30-1, 65, *92*
specific methodology, 5
stakeholders, perceptions of quality, 40
sticky (Post-it) notes, 33-4, 53, 61
strengths, of template analysis, 88-91
structure
of template organisation, 89-90
see also coding structure
study design types, 10-11
sub-themes, 35, 54, *62-5*
subjectivity, 17-18, 19, 20, 22, 59-60
subtle realism, 18
Symon, G., 40
synchronous online interviews, 8

template analysis
approach to building coding structure, 6-7,
25-6
approach to inductive-deductive
reasoning, 6
in context of business and management
research, 7-12
in context of qualitative analysis, 4
core features of, 89
flexibility of, 25-6, 87-8, 89
as generic approach, 5-6, 86
history of, 2-3

template analysis *cont.*
  implications of philosophical position, 16,
      17-19, 20-1, 22-3
  key advice for using, *91-3*
  limitations and challenges, 85-8
  strengths and opportunities, 88-91
  see also case examples of template analysis
template analysis procedures, 3-4, 25-6, 87
  application and development, 4, 35-7, 53-4,
      60, 65-7, 89, *92-3*
  clustering, 3, 33-4, 53, 61
  familiarization with data, 3, 27, 49, 60
  final interpretation, 4, 37-8, 57, 67, 88
  initial templates, 3, 34-5, 51-2, 61-5, 89, *92*
  preliminary coding, 3, 27-33, 49-51, 60-1
  quality assurance, 39-41, 52, 61, 67,
      76-7, 81-3
  writing up, 4, 42-5, 57, 67, *93*
templates
  application and development of, 4, 35-7,
      53-4, 60, 65-7, 89, *92-3*
  final, *4*, 54-7, 67-71, *93*
  initial, 3, 34-5, 51-2, 61-5, 89, *92*
  presentation of, 42-5, *93*
  repurposing, 36
thematic analysis, 2
  key features, 5-7
  relationship with template analysis, 4
thematic presentation of findings, 42
themes
  a priori see a priori themes
  connections between, 35, 38, 54

themes *cont.*
  in final template, 54-7
  in group interviews, 8
  hierarchical organisation of, 34-5
  identifying/modifying, 28, 35, 52, 54, 61-5
  integrative, 35, 54
  patterns of distribution, 37
  prioritising, 37-8
  relationship with codes, 28-9
theoretical position, *91*
  see also a priori themes
thick description, *41*
Tomkins, L., 8
transcription, 7, 27
transferability, 82
transparency, 90-1
  see also audit trail
trustworthiness criteria, 82

Vaag, J., 80
validity, 39-40

Weber, M., 14
well-being (case example), 74, *76*, 79, 81
Wilde, D., 32-3
word processing programs, 27-8, 30-1, 65
work participation and back pain, case example,
    48-58
writing up, 4, 42-5, 57, 67, *93*
written accounts, 8-9
  see also documentary data
Wyatt, M., 75, 77, 79, 80, 81, 82

Fold a Crayfish

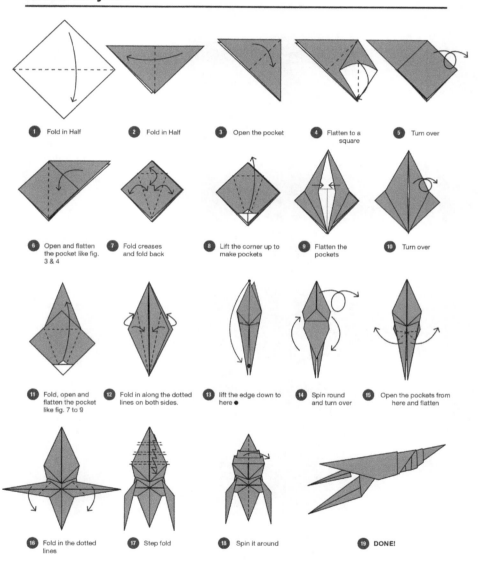

1. Fold in Half

2. Fold in Half

3. Open the pocket

4. Flatten to a square

5. Turn over

6. Open and flatten the pocket like fig. 3 & 4

7. Fold creases and fold back

8. Lift the corner up to make pockets

9. Flatten the pockets

10. Turn over

11. Fold, open and flatten the pocket like fig. 7 to 9

12. Fold in along the dotted lines on both sides.

13. lift the edge down to here ●

14. Spin round and turn over

15. Open the pockets from here and flatten

16. Fold in the dotted lines

17. Step fold

18. Spin it around

19. DONE!